# RECLAIMING FRIENDSHIP

To
my colleagues

Brian and Parames Blacker
Richard and Dawn Brohier
Adrian and Ophelia de Visser
Tony and Cal Senewiratne
Suri and Shanthi Williams

with gratitude for friendship

# RECLAIMING FRIENDSHIP

## *RELATING TO EACH OTHER IN A FALLEN WORLD*

# AJITH FERNANDO

*Cynthia*

*May God lead you to his niche for you*

*Ajith Fernando*

*July '92*

**INTER-VARSITY PRESS**

INTER-VARSITY PRESS
*38 De Montfort Street, Leicester LE1 7GP, England*

**British Library Cataloguing in Publication Data**
Fernando, Ajith
Reclaiming friendship.
1. Christian life. friendship
I. Title
248. 4

ISBN 0-85110-859-8
Set in Linotron Garamond
Photoset by Parker Typesetting Service, Leicester
Printed in Great Britain by Cox & Wyman Ltd, Reading

*Inter-Varsity Press is the book-publishing division of the
Universities and Colleges Christian Fellowship (formerly the
Inter-Varsity Fellowship), a student movement linking
Christian Unions in universities and colleges throughout the
United Kingdom and the Republic of Ireland, and a member
movement of the International Fellowship of Evangelical
Students. For information about local and national activities
write to UCCF, 38 De Montfort Street, Leicester LE1 7GP.*

# CONTENTS

# INTRODUCTION

Much of the work on this book was done while I was on a writing sabbatical at Gordon-Conwell Theological Seminary in America, working on a book on the doctrine of eternal punishment. Almost at the start of the sabbatical I spoke on the topic of 'Team Ministry' at a leadership seminar held at the Seminary and organized by Dr Leighton Ford and Dr Bob Reccord. I was somewhat surprised by the positive response to this talk. A series of Bible expositions I gave at an 'East Coast Ingathering' organized by 'Jews For Jesus' provided me with further opportunity to reflect on the topic of friendship. The organizers asked me to teach on 'Personal Relationships' from the book of Proverbs. An invitation to do an even longer series of messages with the staff of British Youth for Christ helped me delve into the material even further. Since returning to Sri Lanka I have taught this material to many groups of Christians, mostly in Youth for Christ.

On this my first extended stay in the West since my student days in the 70s, I was gripped by a growing concern about the way Christian groups have adopted some models of community life that I believe violate the biblical teaching about how the body of Christ should operate. The thinking of Christians about friendship and inter-personal relationships seems to have been dangerously influenced by the thinking of the world. As a result Christians are missing the enrichment that God intended them to get from friendship, and many are being hurt because of the way they have been treated by the groups they have been connected with. This added a sense of urgency to my work on this book.

I received much stimulation from an international study commission of Youth for Christ which dealt with the issue of 'Human Resource Development' and arrived at conclusions similar to those described in this book. What you have here is actually a study of Christian community life, and a key feature is relationships of accountability, to which we have given the name friendships.

As I proceeded with my study of Proverbs I realized that the antidote to a lot of the problems I saw was found in the insights about friendship given in Proverbs. So I decided to share what I learned with a bigger audience in the form of a book.

In contemporary society many people, in search of what they call 'self-fulfilment', have concluded that costly commitment to others is an unnecessary and bothersome encumbrance. I will show in this book that costly commitment is no such thing. In fact, it is a great aid to the only kind of self-fulfilment that really matters. God has chosen to give some of his richest blessings to us through our loving service and commitment to others

It is most appropriate that I dedicate this book on friendship to my five senior colleagues and their wives in Youth for Christ in Sri Lanka. They have been my team members in the ministry from periods of thirteen to twenty years. Two of them are no longer on staff with us, but their friendship and support continue to be as warm as ever. The contribution of these, my friends, to my growth as a Christian and minister is impossible to describe adequately. They have taught me much of what I know about ministry. It has been my privilege to share with a larger audience, through my writing, what we have learned together as a ministering community. So, in a sense, this book describes some of the scriptural principles of community life that we have experienced together.

In the past few months, our staff team has realized afresh how very important a close community life is, as we seek to serve Christ in a land torn by violence and strife that is sometimes frightening to live amidst. Yet I must say that a lot of what we have learned has been through mistakes we have made. Our experience of community life has not been without its fair share of serious problems.

I must also mention the community of the Nugegoda Methodist Church. My wife and I have served on the leadership team there for the past ten years and our lives have been greatly enriched through that experience.

I wish to acknowledge my gratitude to Dr Christy and Betty Wilson, Prof. Gary and Norma Bekker, Miss Nairy Ohanian and Peter and Louise Burton from the community at Gordon-Conwell Theological Seminary. They became our friends and helped me and my family in so many ways when we were 'strangers in a strange land'.

This is the first book I have written on a computer. It made it so much easier to develop the original expositions into a book. I am grateful to Jack and Lisa Alexander who gave me this computer without ever having met me, based on an appeal from their friend and mine, Jayson Kyle.

The introduction to a book on friendship would be incomplete without reference to my best friend and companion in life, Nelun, and our children, Nirmali and Asiri. They brought so much brightness to my life as I tried to teach a class, write two books and work on checking a new translation of the Sinhala Bible – all on a six-month sabbatical!

I have written this book in a way that would meet the needs of a Christian seeking to read a devotional book. The form is thus expositional. The material is also suited for group study. In the appendix, I have included some material that is particularly applicable to leaders and 'full-time' Christian workers.

In addition to the passages from Proverbs, I decided to use the famous text on friendship from Ecclesiastes, which, like Proverbs, belongs to the Wisdom Literature. Yet this book should not be viewed as a 'study' of Proverbs. What I have tried to do is study carefully some texts in Proverbs and Ecclesiastes and glean insights from them about friendship and then apply these insights to our contemporary experience.

11

I need to express my indebtedness to the commentaries on Proverbs that were always by my side as I worked on this book and which are listed at the back. I was especially helped by the commentaries of Kenneth Aitken, Robert Alden, Charles Bridges, Derek Kidner and Charles Martin. Stephen Voorwinde's *Wisdom for Today's Issues*, a topical arrangement of the Proverbs, was also a very helpful resource. I came across Gary Inrig's fine book, *Quality Friendship*, only as I was coming to the end of writing this book. It contains many good insights on the biblical teaching about friendship.

I send this book out with the prayer that it will help many Christians to resist the contemporary cultural trend away from establishing lasting and committed ties with others. I pray that many would be encouraged to form close Christian friendships and, through that, experience the enrichment that God intended us to have.

# CHAPTER ONE

# FRIENDS AND REAL FRIENDS

When I was in my late teens and early twenties I belonged to a small group of Youth for Christ volunteers who met regularly for fellowship. We usually met on Sunday nights, and talked for hours about issues that related to our lives and the ministry we were involved in. We shared our problems and joys, we discussed, we debated and we prayed.

Some of that original group are still active in Youth for Christ. Others are active in churches and different organizations. But still, when we meet, it does not take us long before we experience again the joy of Christian friendship. During those times together ties had developed that were based on truth. Such ties do not dissolve during years of separation, unless we reject the truth that was the foundation of the friendship.

This is quite a contrast to some of the friendships I had when I was a schoolboy. These too were close friendships; but only for a time. I am usually very happy to meet old school friends now, but after some time there isn't much to talk about. Those were temporary friendships because they were based on things that did not last.

My experiences with that group of Youth for Christ volunteers in the crucial years of my spiritual growth remind me of an incident from John Wesley's early life, recorded in his journal. He once met a person, whom he calls a 'serious man', who told him, 'Sir, you wish to serve God and go to heaven? Remember that you cannot serve him alone. You must therefore find companions or make them. The Bible knows nothing of solitary religion.' Wesley never forgot that wise counsel. Much later he said, 'Christianity is a social religion. To turn it into a solitary religion is indeed to destroy it.'

One of the great contributions of the early Methodist movement was to bring back the practice found in the early church of spiritual accountability. With the recent rise of individualism in the church, there seems to be a need to emphasize afresh this biblical understanding of community life. I hope to do so in this book by taking principles about friendship from the Bible and seeing how they apply today. We will start with an important affirmation of the nature of friendship, found in Proverbs.

## TWO TYPES OF FRIENDS

A man of many companions may come to ruin, but there is a friend who sticks closer than a brother.

(Proverbs 18:24)

The form of this proverb is typical of Hebrew poetry which usually has two statements that are related to each other in some way. This is called parallelism. In this verse the two statements give converse truths.

The first line has been understood in various ways. The rendering in the Authorized Version, 'A man that has friends must show himself friendly', is most certainly wrong. The basic idea seems to be that there are two types of friends. The different translations give the sense of what the first group of friends is like. The NIV renders it, 'A man of many companions may come to ruin', emphasizing how dangerous this type of friendship is. The RSV offers a reason why these friendships are dangerous: 'There are friends who pretend to be friends.' Whatever the exact meaning, this line points out that we could have acquaintances who are not real friends.

The second statement in this couplet describes 'a friend who sticks closer than a brother'. The word 'sticks' is the same word used of a man cleaving to his wife (Genesis 2:24), of Ruth clinging to her mother-in-law, Naomi (Ruth 1:14) and of Israel cleaving to the Lord (Deuteronomy 10:20; 11:22, etc.). It has the sense of clinging to someone in affection and loyalty.* These two ideas of affection and loyalty are the key to true friendship.

The use of the word 'brother' in comparing the value of friendship is significant. Many converts to Christianity have had the pain of being alienated by their family members because of their faith. We

*Harris, R. Laird, Archer, Gleason L., Waltke, Bruce K., eds, *Theological Wordbook of the Old Testament* (Chicago: Moody Press, 1980), p. 178.

must never give up trying to mend these family relationships. Indeed, if we continue to show love and loyalty to the family despite the rejection, after some time the relationship may be restored. But in the meantime, God does compensate, first by his comforting presence, and then through the friendship of fellow Christians. And, as this verse tells us, the closeness of these friends could be even more intimate than that of family members, for they stick 'closer than a brother'.

There are then two types of friends: acquaintances and real friends. Derek Kidner in his commentary on Proverbs, says, 'Proverbs ... is emphatic that a few close friends are better than a host of acquaintances, and stand in a class by themselves' (page 44). Jesus showed this in his life. He ministered to the crowds, but he had a group of special friends, the twelve disciples, and from among them the inner circle of three and from them the 'disciple whom Jesus loved'.

## FRIENDS VERSUS CLIQUES

Jesus, however, was not cliquish. Cliques form when people are friendly purely for selfish reasons. Because of the selfish motivation behind the friendship, cliques often separate from those they see as a threat. They reject people, and when the members of the clique are together they often speak ill and gossip about others. In contrast, the small group that Jesus had was a ministering community. Their mission was to serve people. Receiving strength from the fellowship, they gave themselves to minister to people's needs in a very sacrificial way. So we are not advocating a clique here. Cliques alienate people. Biblical friendships serve people.

To those involved in ministry, I may mention that we must seek ways to dispel the misconception that we are concerned only about our 'close friends'. This is a criticism often levelled against those who practise close community life. One way of dealing with this problem is to abstain from talking only with these friends when we are at public gatherings. It is best to use these times to express friendship with those we are not that close to. We should try to let the others in the congregation, or whatever group we lead, know that these, our 'team members', are people who have joined in to help in service and are willing to pay the price of the commitment required of them. They are our team and not our clique.

## ALIEN TO OUR CULTURE

Our cultural environment is not very conducive to the type of close relationships which Proverbs advocates. People are very friendly today – friendly with a lot of people! But when you are a friend to a lot of people, it is possible not to be a close friend to anybody.

We get so used to 'small talk' that it can be hard to stop and give time for serious and honest talk. Besides, ours is a generation of 'busy-bodies'. We enjoy going from place to place and keeping ourselves active all the time. Busy-bodies find it a strain to concentrate when someone else is pouring out his or her heart. When the person talking realizes this, he or she will stop sharing. By our inability to give time to listen we make it impossible for close friendships to develop.

The idea of lasting commitment (which we'll come back to later) has also gone out of fashion. With it has gone the possibility of true friendship, an important feature of which is commitment.

## Friendship and truth

One of the keys to a deep friendship is time spent in long conversations. This is the type of relationship that Jesus had with his friends, the disciples, as the gospels show. He said, 'I have called you friends, for everything that I learned from my Father I have made known to you' (John 15:15). At the heart of the friendship was the communication of truth.

While Proverbs may not expressly state the value of extended conversations, it implies it. Deep conversation is how the company of the wise can operate (see pp. 19–21). Deep conversation is how the wisdom that comes from friends is mediated (see chapter six).

Many of us don't seem to have time for such long conversations. We have so many things to do! When we have free time, it is spent on entertainment. Leisure time is packed with trips to the beach, vacations and the like. Even when we are with friends, we want to be active, go somewhere, play a game, watch a film or whatever.

Most of us can't bear the thought of just sitting and discussing issues. If we need information we can get it from an encyclopaedia or a book. Speed-reading techniques have made it possible for us to absorb facts much quicker than through long, time-consuming discussions. So the discussions we have are generally confined to pragmatic issues where a decision has to be made, or to entertaining topics like humour, sports or current events.

The problem with this situation is that we are simply getting information into our minds without interacting with the facts, without asking how or what we are going to do with what we read. We are producing technicians with lots of facts, not thinkers. Thinkers have depth. And depth has a richness to it. It satisfies the deep desire in our hearts implanted by a God who is committed to truth. His understanding of truth includes more than facts. Christian truth has a qualitative and experiential aspect to it. So truth can be enjoyed only if we are willing to linger with it, to ask what its implications are, to ask how it should influence our thinking and our acting. Is it any wonder that our generation does not know the joy of truth spoken of so much in the Psalms?

Those who will set apart time for enriching discussions on issues, on the things of God, will rediscover the joy of truth. Through that they will find a new depth of true personal fulfilment. This, then, is a plea to bring back long 'chats' into our schedules, to give significant slots of time to truth-related discussions. Truth is one of the richest aspects of the Christian life and so it should be one of the richest aspects of Christian fellowship.

Proverbs 15:31 says,

He who listens to a life-giving rebuke
  will be at home among the wise.

The expression 'at home among the wise' implies that there is such a thing as a fellowship of wise people – people committed to the pursuit of knowledge. A key feature of friendship must be the quest for a deeper understanding of truth. This, as we said earlier, is the type of fellowship that Jesus had with his disciples. The gospels give a significant amount of space to his dialogues on truth with them.

I have found that truth-related dialogues have caused me a considerable amount of inconvenience in terms of my schedule. Most of them are not previously planned, they simply emerge during an ordinary conversation. But that inconvenience has been a price worth paying, for through these conversations I have received knowledge which has refreshed and enriched me. As Proverbs 2:10 says,

> Wisdom will enter your heart,
>> and knowledge will be pleasant to your
>> soul.

Anyone who takes the call of Christ seriously today will soon encounter a basically selfish approach to life, which is so contrary to the Christian way. In face of this it is very encouraging to meet others who also follow the path of discipleship. The presence of common convictions amidst the confusion of today's world is an important ingredient of Christian friendship. As C. S. Lewis puts it in his book *The Four Loves*, 'Friendship . . . is born at the moment when one says to another "What! you too? I thought that no-one but myself . . ."' (page 92). The presence of people who seem to understand, gives us the courage to persevere along our chosen path of non-conformity.

We are not advocating a club of intellectual snobs, who think that because they belong to the company of the wise they are superior to others. The key to entering this company is teachability. It is the one 'who listens to a life-giving rebuke' who, 'will be at home with the wise'. Those who are proud of their intelligence are always trying to show how wise they are. They cannot have true fellowship. Those who belong to the fellowship of wise people want to learn from each other. So intense is their desire to do this that they are very open to rebuke from others.

This is the type of relationship the Old Testament advocates that parents have with their children. Parents should talk with their children about truth. They are the first to teach them the basics of the Jewish faith. Fathers have a big part to play in this (see Proverbs 1:8–9; 4:1–6; 6:20–24). There are interesting provisions made in the Jewish rituals for children to ask questions of their parents. For example, stones are placed as a memorial of the crossing of the Jordan, with the express purpose of provoking a question from children. This would, in turn, provide parents with an opportunity to relate the story of God's great act (Joshua 4:1–9). An important part of the Passover ritual was when a son asked the father, 'How is this night different from other nights?' Similarly today some of the most useful times that parents can have with their children are times spent discussing issues. This is one of the keys to developing meaningful friendships between parents and children.

The point, then, is that the quest to understand truth should be a key aspect of Christian interpersonal relationships. Today's activity orientated society, shown in its love-affair with quick, tangible results, may make this difficult to do. The problem has become so serious that I heard a leading American theologian once say that it has become almost impossible for America to develop fresh theology. He thinks society has become so pragmatically oriented that it is becoming difficult for people to think in terms of truth categories. The result of such pragmatism is an emptiness which truth alone can fill. Those who give the time to truth-related discussions will be richly rewarded with 'the fullness of truth' which is vital for the fulfilment of human beings who have been made in the image of the God of truth.

Christians all over the world are indebted to C. S. Lewis for the great wisdom he made available to the church through his writings. He was a person who had many friends. He had what biographers call his 'inner circle' made up of friends such as Arthur Greeves, Owen Barfield, and his wife, Joy Davidman. George Sayer in his book *Jack: C. S. Lewis and his Times* makes it clear these people had much to do with the developing of C. S. Lewis' great insights.

It would be good to end this section on 'Friendship and truth' with a description of this type of meeting of friends. This classic statement on friendship appears in Lewis' book, *The Four Loves*:

He is lucky beyond desert to be in such company. Especially when the whole group is together, each bringing out all that is best, wisest, or funniest in all the others. Those are the golden sessions; when four of us after a hard days walking have come to our inn; when our slippers are on, our feet spread out toward the blaze and our drinks at our elbows; when the whole world, and something beyond the world, opens itself to our minds as we talk; and no-one has any claim on or any responsibility for another, but all are freemen and equals as if

22

we had first met an hour ago, while at the same time an affection mellowed by the years enfolds us. Life – natural life – has no better gift to give. Who could have deserved it.

## The importance of learning to linger

The type of friendship we are advocating is rare today because we live in an age that has forgotten how to linger. Time is too precious we say, to waste it lingering. Time *is* precious, but that is not why we don't linger. Our problem is that we are too restless.

We don't know what it is to be silent before God. We don't know what it is to meditate on truth. Similarly we don't know what it is to spend long periods in conversation with friends. It is in such times that minds meet, that we experience together the joy of truth, which is one of the most precious forms of joy. People who make the sacrifice of letting long conversation time eat into their schedules – and that is a sacrifice – will know the joy of minds meeting on a deeper level. From this, deep relationships of true friendship will be forged.

Jesus was willing to make that sacrifice. When Andrew and another of the disciples of John asked Jesus where he was staying, he did not simply give them the information they wanted. He said, 'Come and see.' They went with him 'and spent that day with him' (John 1:37–39), that is, the remainder of it from about 4 p.m. (See Leon Morris' book, *Reflections on the Gospel of John*, page 77.) The Saviour of the world, the perfect model for the Christian leader, acted in a way that seemed quite out of place for a key leader, according to much of modern thinking about management. He spent many hours on an unplanned appointment!

Most people today would say that they don't have time for this type of extended contact with people. So friendship has become something cheap and shallow. Like many other words, friendship has lost its original meaning and what we have is a diluted understanding. Inflation has hit not only the economic scene, it has hit the area of inter-personal relationships also!

Take the practice of shaking hands. This seems to have originated as the sign of a blood covenant, when a pledge would be taken that one would protect another's life. This pledge would be sealed by the clasping of hands and the shedding of blood. How far this meaning is from today's!

Further evidence of the inflation that has taken place in our understanding of friendship is what we mean today by the word 'friendly'. To us a friendly person is one who makes acquaintances easily, the 'life and soul' of a party. While this quality is not necessarily a bad one, very often these so-called friendly people don't have many deep friends. They have a lot of superficial acquaintances, which is not a bad thing, but they have no close friends, which is a bad thing.

## THE MARRIAGE RELATIONSHIP

The problem of not having time for extended conversations has also affected the husband-wife relationship in many families. Before marriage there would be those 'dates' which provided so many opportunities for conversation. But after the wedding the couple comes 'back to reality' and gets on with the business of living. There are so many things to do. The children take up so much energy, especially from the wife. Where is the time for long conversations? But without them, couples get distant. However much they may love each other, they can't remain best friends unless they communicate in an extended way. And isn't that what couples are supposed to be: best friends?

My wife and I have found that the best time for us to talk like this is after the children have gone to bed. We may have to stay up into the night to do so. We are often quite tired the next day. But we're happy! Hearts have communicated, and that brings immense satisfaction. It also gives security.

We live in a world where people are competing and struggling to overtake each other. It is good to know that there are some people who will accept us for what we are, and in whose presence we can 'let our hair down', be ourselves and talk about things that really matter to us.

We conclude by repeating a fact that has recurred over and over again in this chapter. True friendship calls for time – time to talk.

# CHAPTER TWO

# TEAM MINISTRY

In the previous chapter we discussed some of the implications of the statement in Proverbs 18:24, that 'there is a friend who sticks closer than a brother'. Jesus' relationship with his disciples is a good example of this type of close friendship, and their relationship can be described best as a ministering team.

## NEW TESTAMENT MINISTRY TEAMS

There is a lot of evidence in the New Testament that team ministry is God's chosen way for people to operate. It is only in exceptional cases, like that of Philip the evangelist, that we see ministry being done alone in the New Testament. And even in the case of Philip, we cannot say with certainty that he went to Samaria by himself. It seems clear, however, that he was alone when he met the Ethiopian eunuch.

When Jesus sent out his twelve apostles for ministry, they were sent two by two (Mark 6:7). This was also the case with the seventy-two disciples who went on a ministry tour in twos (Luke 10:1). When Peter stood up to speak on the day of Pentecost we are told he 'stood up with the Eleven' (Acts 2:14).When he talks of his witness he says, 'We are witnesses of these things' (Acts 2:32; 3:15; 5:32). He was not a lone voice, but part of the ministering team that was backing him as he preached. Therefore we see Peter and John ministering as a team (Acts 3:1, 4; 4:1, 23; 8:14). When Peter went to the home of Cornelius on his historic visit, he took six brothers with him (Acts 10:23; 11:12).

The Holy Spirit, commissioning the first missionary team in the history of the church, says, 'Set apart for me Barnabas and Saul ...' (Acts 13:2). When they separate, both Paul and Barnabas take others along with them. And we know that Paul almost never travelled alone. He had his famous travelling 'Bible school' where he trained his 'interns' like Timothy and Titus. Even when he was taken to Rome as a prisoner, Luke was with him (Acts 27:2). In his last letter written from prison he told Timothy, 'Do your best to come to me quickly ... only Luke is with me. Get Mark and bring him with you, because he is helpful to me in my ministry' (2 Timothy 4:9, 11).

So we can safely say that team ministry is the normal style of ministry in the Bible. As we go on we will see that there are very good reasons for this. Let me say here that we should be very careful about sending a person on a ministry assignment alone, especially when we are starting a work in a new area. The pitfalls and discouragements of pioneering work are so intense that it would be good to make sure that those who go to start a new work go as a team.

## TEAMS ARE MORE EFFECTIVE

Perhaps the best known passage in the Scriptures on the value of a team is Ecclesiastes 4:9–12. Most of the affirmations in this passage will be studied in chapter nine, 'The comfort of friends'. Here we will discuss only the first affirmation:

> Two are better than one
>     because they have a good return for their
>         work.
>
> (Ecclesiastes 4:9)

The feature mentioned here is the productivity of a team. When different people contribute to a project, the gifts of each person are used and so the result is much richer.

This is the thrust of 1 Corinthians 12:12–31, the great passage on gifts, where Paul compares the church to a human body, both with many different members. Much has been written on this subject so I do not need to dwell on it here.

A helpful illustration of the value of differing gifts is of a team preparing for an evangelistic rally. A gifted artist designs an attractive handbill. Committed people use the handbill when inviting friends to the programme. Smiling welcomers make the non-Christians who come feel accepted at the meeting. The musicians present the gospel in a very attractive way. The person who shares her testimony shows what Christ can do in someone's life. The preacher faithfully proclaims the message. The counsellor helps the inquirer to commit his or her life to Christ. And the local church provides nurture for the new Christian. A great preacher, who did not have the type of body-backing described above, would in the long run be less effective than a preacher with half his ability, who had the backing of a team of committed people.

A particular benefit of team life which is not mentioned very often is the way team members help to bring out the best in us. Our ideas are often refined and improved when there is the input of others. Sometimes there may be tensions because of this, but the end product is so much better. Proverbs 27:17 describes this beautifully:

> As iron sharpens iron,
>   so one man sharpens another.

Team members are most effective in sharpening each other when they are not all alike. This seems to have been the case in the church in Antioch which had an effective ministry of evangelism, pastoral care, relief and missions: 'In the church at Antioch there were prophets and teachers' (Acts 13:1).

Prophets are visionaries who provide special guidance directly from the Lord for specific situations. Today, because we have a completed Bible, the prophetic gift is not so common in the church as in the first century. However, we can see no convincing evidence in the Scriptures that this gift has been taken away from the church, as some claim. Though the specific gift of prophesy may be less prominent, we need prophetic voices in the church. They may not exercise the classic gift of prophecy, but their prophetic insight will direct

God's people into new areas of involvement. It will also lead to questioning the validity of some revered traditions and practices that may be no longer appropriate. We can call these people radicals because they go to the roots of issues and suggest drastic changes. We need such radicals in the church. I do not refer to theological radicals who deviate from the truth revealed in the Scriptures. We do not need that type of radicalism in the church. The radicals we need are people who suggest change as they see the way the authoritative Word of God applies to specific situations.

Teachers on the other hand expound the Scriptures. They focus attention on the unchanging foundations of the Word of God. As their focus is on foundational principles, they are usually more conservative in their emphases.

A healthy team will have both radicals and conservatives. Usually when these two types are found in the same group there will be a lot of friction. The radicals struggle to have patience with the conservatives, because the latter are careful to ensure that new schemes are not a departure from orthodoxy. Often they give up trying to work with the team and work alone instead. But they achieve much less that way.

Conservatives, on the other hand, don't often make an effort to understand the radicals. They either get the radicals to leave the group or they leave themselves. But again their ministries will not make much progress because of the lack of 'ideas folk' in their group.

When radicals and conservatives work together under a common commitment to the authority of Scripture, there will be responsible growth: the radicals ensure there will be growth, the conservatives ensure it will be responsible growth.

For example, visionaries, consumed with a passion to complete a task they have begun, may sometimes be tempted to bend certain rules in order to get the job done quickly. The teachers, with their focus on the principles, will object to the breaking of the rules, and ensure that the growth is responsible.

The end result is a team that can achieve much more than a group of people who always agree on everything.

Similarly a person with a managerial orientation can help Christian groups to maintain responsible growth. I have heard criticism of the 'accountant type' of person, because they are said to stifle growth and creativity. Yet I am convinced that if such people work in the context of a team, they can make an invaluable contribution to a work.

We have an accountant, Chandran Williams, who, as part of our leadership team, manages our administrative and financial operations, as a volunteer. There have been times when I have gone to him excitedly for funds to purchase some piece of equipment which I feel confident is exactly what we need for our work. Often Chandran suggests we delay making the purchase until he does a study of our needs and of what is available in the market. I find this taxing on my patience, but how grateful I am that we waited for his wise counsel and bought what was best for us, and not what I got excited about!

Sometimes a leader may feel that a particular project is very urgent, and attempt to use funds that were designated for something else, promising, of course, to pay back the money. Accountants usually object to such a procedure. Then there are certain projects which require large sums of money to set up and will continue to require a substantial amount to maintain. Because we have raised the initial investment that is necessary to start off, we may launch out on the project. But we may not have made adequate plans for raising the funds needed to maintain the project. Accountants usually object to this procedure too. But often, caught up by the excitement of the project, we ignore these objections and go ahead. How many churches and organizations have got into serious difficulties because they did not heed the warnings of the 'accountant types'. In a team, the accountant and the visionary could harmonize beautifully to produce responsible growth that honours God.

## FRIENDSHIP AT TEAM MEETINGS

The term 'team' is used in a broad sense in this book to mean a group of people who have come together with a common goal in mind. It may be used for the different groups in a church or an organization. Examples are those involved together in a ministry project like the youth fellowship committee or the board, the team of staff workers and the senior leaders. These teams need to be groups where people practise the Christian art of friendship. But while ministering to others outside the team, team members should concentrate on those they minister to, not on each other, otherwise the team will become a clique. The team meetings should be the place to express their friendship and to minister to each other.

These meetings usually are times when the team gets together to evaluate, plan and discuss problems – that is, to discuss business. But this business is Christian ministry. It must be done using the Christian model of ministry. This is the body-life model. I fear that most of our board and team meetings follow a secular business model, rather than the body-life model. (I said a *secular* business model because there may be businesses which use models that are compatible with the Christian model.) The meeting would commence with the ritual opening prayer and close with the benediction. Once in a while the business would be punctuated by a testimony or a ministry report. The rest of the time, however, 'Robert's Rules of Order' seemed more influential in directing the style of the meeting (though hopefully not the substance discussed) than the Bible.

Let me explain. The key to the body-life model is the spiritual union that the members have first with Christ and, through that, with each other. A key expression of this spiritual union is being of one mind. This idea is well expressed in the book of Acts where the Greek word *homothumadon* is used many times to describe the life of the early church. This word has been translated 'of one mind', 'of one accord' and 'as one man'. (The NIV's 'together' is possible in some of the instances of its use, but is too weak a translation for most of these instances.) The word describes a group of people who are knit together with a common purpose. Sometimes the word is used to describe people who were together in a common commitment to Christ (Acts 1:14; 2:46; 4:24; 5:12; *cf.* Romans 15:6). Sometimes the word is used to describe the way the opponents of the gospel got together to battle against the church (Acts 7:57; 18:12; 19:29). The idea then is of a uniting passion.

This type of bonding is not easy to achieve, especially when the group consists of leaders who generally have strong feelings about the way things should be done. Most often it comes out of an atmosphere of worship and frankness. The worship helps to affirm the basis of the unity, which is our common link with Christ. The frankness helps to maintain the unity in experience. But when leaders are frank, usually a lot of sparks fly. The discussion sometimes gets quite heated as each one presents what he or she feels so strongly about.

I have been part of the Youth for Christ leadership team for about twenty-four years. During these years we have had a lot of times of friction, sometimes even resulting in tears. Yet we have found that all our 'love fights' have ended in resolution, though sometimes the resolution took a while to emerge. After the resolution has come and we have prayed together, we sense that we are deeper in our love for each other and understanding of each other than before the battle. In fact, often the battle starts because we had drifted apart. Most frequently the drifting apart occurred because we had not met each other as we should have, due to our heavy schedules. The battle was a means which God used to get us back together.

The situation becomes more complex if some of those at the meeting are not walking in full fellowship with each other. Body theology demands that these issues be ironed out before biblical ministry is done. A considerable time must be given for the 'love fight' which is aimed at resolving the differences. But the unity that is forged after the resolution is very deep and the ensuing ministry of this team is spiritually very powerful. In fact, the meeting may proceed at a very fast speed after the correct spiritual climate has been created because the group is in tune with God and with each other.

Is the structure of our board meetings and team meetings able to accommodate such love fights? Most often the answer is no. Let me give an example. The chairman has invited a rich donor to attend the meeting as an observer. The staff do not feel free to be frank in this person's presence. But the rich donor is very impressed by the programme being planned and makes a large donation to the work. There is great rejoicing over this and the decision to invite the person is 'proved' to have been a wise one.

An impressive programme is launched using this money. But the programme is administered by a team that is not of one accord. There are impressive statistics to show the way the money was used, but the programme has made little contribution to the growth of the kingdom of God. The buildings bought with the money or the materials produced are not recorded in the annals of the eternal kingdom. It was work done in the flesh. It lacked God's blessing because it sidestepped God's requirements for effective service. People mistakenly assumed that the models effective in producing temporal success would also produce eternal success.

One of the biggest scandals in the life of the church in the second half of the twentieth century is the high input in terms of human resources, time and money that has produced a minimal impact from the perspective of eternity. This is because the work was not done in God's way.

I wish to make it clear that I am not advocating meetings that drag on with different people rambling about things that are of no relevance. Team members in the body-life model of ministry are *homothumadon* people. They are fired by a unifying passion to achieve some goals for the kingdom. Passionate people will not tolerate rambling. Their urgency will cause them to challenge all unnecessary conversation so that they can give themselves to the task in hand.

Our plea then is for Christian groups to return to the body-life model of ministry. It may result in what is seen as an inefficient use of meeting time. But if we free ourselves from this bondage to time, which produces technical excellence without the depth and the power of spiritual penetration, we will realize that what is most important is not the volume of work we do, but the amount of lasting impact we make.

An implication of what we have said above is that we must seek to foster unanimity in the team about a given project. While this may not be directly implied in a text from Proverbs, it is certainly implied in the Acts of the Apostles. In fact 'unanimity' is the essential meaning of the word *homothumadon*.* Its use in connection with meetings is seen in Acts 15:25, 'So we all agreed to choose some men and send them to you . . .'. At the end of the controversial Jerusalem conference,

*See E. D. Schmitz, 'Unanimity', *The New International Dictionary of New Testament Theology*, Vol.3, ed., Colin Brown (Exeter: The Paternoster Press and Grand Rapids: Zondervan Publishing House, 1978), pp. 908–909.

those attending were unanimous about the choice of the team of people who were to take the letter from the conference to the Gentile churches. There had been a lot of debate, but at the end unanimity was achieved.

Today, however, we do not approach differences of opinion at meetings in this way. We don't have time for debates. We aren't used to being frank with each other. Thus disagreeing will be an awkward thing to do. So sometimes we opt for taking a vote, then the decision of the majority prevails. Other times we say something like, 'I don't agree with this plan of yours. But that's your business. So you go ahead and do it.' That may sound generous, but there is no *homothumadon*-type oneness in the team. So what we may call 'body power' will be lacking from the project. The dissenter will not back his colleague with all his heart. When the project goes through hard times, as most projects do at some time, the lack of enthusiasm of the dissenter will cause others (who are struggling with discouragement over the problems being faced) to be demotivated. If the project goes wrong the dissenter will say something like, 'I thought as much.' But by refusing to speak, the dissenter has hurt the body. His approach may have helped the body to take a decision quickly, but he has hurt this body in the process. Some keep quiet so that there will be peace. The fear of causing what we may call 'constructive unrest' comes from a lack of commitment to the body and from spiritual lethargy. It must be roundly condemned.

The project would have been carried out with so much more spiritual power if the whole team had been of one mind about it. But it takes time to achieve such a oneness. Yet that is the price we must pay to have the power of the Holy Spirit in our ministries.

## COLLEAGUES AS FRIENDS

There is a trend today for people to have their close and warm friendships outside the context of their ministering team or their group of colleagues. Some people have their most satisfying experiences of fellowship at week-end retreats where they meet with relative strangers and have very open times of sharing. It is essential that Christians have good friends outside the group to which they are affiliated. This 'outside perspective' can be a source of much enrichment to them. It is also an expression of one's commitment to the total body of Christ which encompasses the whole church. However, these 'outside' friendships must never be a substitute for close friendships with colleagues.

Often people separate the joy of fellowship from the responsibility of on-going commitment to those with whom they live and work closely. So their 'fellowship group' is not the group they work with. They think it is too cumbersome to have the fellowship type of relationship with their colleagues. But this is unnatural and certainly very distant from the fellowship model in Christ's team of disciples and in Paul's teams as described in Acts. Besides, it is those we are close to who can most help us grow. They know us best and can help us daily. It is sometimes uncomfortable to live with this type of helper, but it is so much more effective as an agent for good in our lives.

# CAN LEADERS BE FRIENDS?

When I first taught the material that ultimately became this book, one of the questions asked of me was whether leaders are able to have the type of friendship I was talking about with those they lead. This is a particularly important issue today because leaders are often told they must not have close relationships of this kind. A friend of mine who is a leader in a Christian organization was reprimanded by his director for being too friendly with those working under him. The reason given was that those in managerial positions should keep a distance from the rest of the employees. This seems to be one of those areas where the church has been unduly influenced by the world.

The testimony of Scripture is that the great biblical leaders were very open to intimate friendship with those they led. Jesus is the supreme example of leadership for the Christian, and his relationship with his disciples is the highest example of the value of friendship between leaders and those they lead. In his classic statement about this, Jesus said to his disciples, 'I no longer call you servants, because a servant does not know his master's business. Instead, I have called you friends, for everything that I learned from my Father I have made known to you' (John 15:15). So Jesus related to his disciples as he would to friends.

Paul also led the young Timothy while maintaining a close friendship with him. He did not hesitate to be open about himself before Timothy. He told him, 'You, however, know all about my teaching, my way of life, my purpose, faith, patience, love, endurance, persecutions, sufferings

. . .' (2 Timothy 3:10–11). Timothy knew everything about Paul. Far from keeping his distance, he unashamedly expressed his feelings of affection towards Timothy. He wrote to Timothy, 'I long to see you, so that I may be filled with joy' (2 Timothy 1:4).

Paul was unashamed and unafraid to expose his emotions to the rebellious and often wayward Corinthians also. He wrote to them that even though there was an open door for preaching in Troas he had no peace of mind until Titus came with news of how the Corinthians had received his letter (2 Corinthians 2:12–13). He talked to them about the daily pressure of concern he had for all the churches and of how news from the churches elicited strong emotional reactions in him (2 Corinthians 11:28–29). He also writes: 'We have spoken freely to you, Corinthians, and opened wide our hearts to you. We are not withholding our affection from you, but you are withholding yours from us' (2 Corinthians 6:11–12).

In view of the above it is not surprising that F. F. Bruce, in his book about Paul's friends, *The Pauline Circle*, should say, 'Paul's genius for friendship has been spoken of so often that it has become proverbial – almost cliché.' Bruce says that he 'attracted friends around him as a magnet attracts iron filings' (pages 8–9).

Why then is there so much reluctance today to associate friendship with leadership? One reason may be that we give too high a place to status in our understanding of leadership. As friendship seems to cause one to drop a few rungs in the status scale, it is viewed as a hindrance to effective leadership. We must never forget that the model for biblical

40

leadership is *servanthood*. That has little to do with status and a lot to do with responsibility. Responsibility is not a hindrance to friendship, but status could be.

I believe, however, that the major reason is a more basic one. We live in an age where people have not succeeded in integrating holiness and love. This is causing havoc in the theology and practice of Christians in almost every area of life. Leadership is one of the affected areas. Just as God's nature is characterized by a perfect mingling of holiness and love, leaders also must exemplify this dual nature.

We respond to God's holiness with respect. We 'worship God acceptably with reverence and awe, for our "God is a consuming fire"' (Hebrews 12:28–29). We respond to God's love with intimacy. So 'we have confidence [or boldness] to enter the Most Holy Place' (Hebrews 10:19). In the same way the relationship between a leader and those he or she leads is characterized by respect and intimacy.

But today we seem to find it so difficult to integrate holiness with love. In the East, many fathers are respected by their children, but are aloof from them. In the West, on the other hand, there is a lot of freedom in many families between a father and child. But respect is woefully lacking. This same problem has hit our relationship to God. Is it any surprise then that people have difficulty when it comes to applying the integrated approach to leadership?

How can a leader who is intimate with those he leads win their respect? The answer must be by integrating holiness with love in his relationship with them. I do not need to describe how the love segment of this relationship is manifested. But some explanation on the holiness of the leader is in order.

The first requirement for a leader's holiness is an exemplary life. Paul told the young Timothy, who was having some trouble winning the respect of the members of the church in Ephesus, 'Don't let anyone look down on you because you are young, but set an example for the believers in speech, in life, in love, in faith and in purity' (1 Timothy 4:12). This is a more exacting task than enforcing respect through an organizational chart! But it comes to the heart of Christian leadership which is to lead people into the will of God for the individual and for the organization. And a basic requirement for such leadership is godliness. So Paul urges Timothy to 'train [himself] to be godly' (1 Timothy 4:7).

Just before asking him to be an example, Paul tells Timothy, 'Command and teach these things' (1 Timothy 4:11). These are two other things which build respect. To 'command' is to give clear instructions. Leaders should know where they are going. Out of their contact with God's Word and the issues people face they should be able to guide people through the challenges confronting them. If they don't know how to respond to a crisis, they must, like Moses, seek the face of God and grapple with the issue until they have come up with some idea of how to respond to it. Of course, this grappling must be done in community. But the leader must be involved in it, without handing the job over to an expert, which is what many leaders do today.

Then the leader must teach, says Paul. This is the

supreme ministry activity of Christian leaders. They can't leave the job of teaching to an expert, for biblical leaders lead by teaching. They teach people the truth and ask them to obey the truth. The only ministry-related qualification required of an elder in 1 Timothy 3 is the ability to teach. All the other qualifications are qualities related to the character of the person. How far our ideas of leadership seem to be from Paul's! Our leaders are now essentially administrators who leave the teaching function to others. They have no forum for spiritual respect-building activities. So, naturally, they would be reluctant to participate in intimacy-building activities too.

Then the leader, because of his holiness, must 'correct' and 'rebuke' (2 Timothy 4:2). His intimacy does not prevent him from responding with indignation to error and sin. The ability to encourage and to rebuke is one of the essentials for integrating love and holiness. In fact these two ministries are placed together by Paul in 2 Timothy 4:2. The leader's hatred of wrong will build respect if it is backed by an exemplary life and a loving concern for the wrongdoer.

Through the factors mentioned above, respect will be won almost automatically. If a leader is not a good example, if he does not give direction, if he does not teach and if he does not rebuke, there will be no biblical foundation for the building of respect. Such leaders will have to depend on their status and rank to get respect. They will find it difficult to develop friendships with those 'under them'.

There is, however, one aspect of 'freedom' and 'friendship', common today, which cannot mingle with holiness, and thus with respect. This too, as we shall see, comes from the failure to integrate holiness with love. I refer to the off-colour jokes and unedifying conversations that are often heard when people 'let their hair down'. Even Christians find it hard to joke without leaving the boundaries of purity. If leaders participate in such activities with those they lead, then they will lose the respect of those people. And they deserve to!

So today's leaders don't socialize with those 'under' them. Instead they socialize with their peers and often act in shameful ways at parties and gatherings. If that is the understanding of socializing that people have, then the advice to leaders not to socialize with those under them is understandable. But that is not the way Christian leaders ought to socialize. They ought always to be holy people. Holiness will win the respect of all. And if it is mingled with true concern it will win affection and result in a marked influence for good in the lives of all who have the privilege of being led by them.

# CHAPTER THREE

# FRIENDSHIPS IN A FALLEN WORLD

While Proverbs has a lot to say about friendship, it does not paint a completely rosy picture about the experiences associated with it. Proverbs is well aware that we live in a fallen world tainted everywhere by sin. So it does not ignore the fact that we must be careful about whom we trust and not be surprised when friendships cause us pain and disappointment.

In Proverbs 17:17, for example, there are some lofty words about friends loving constantly and helping out in times of trouble. But the next verse gives a warning about trusting people who are not trustworthy. One of the great things about the wisdom of the Bible is its realism. It presents a life of sacrificial love, but not of foolish love.

That is why the Bible is such a trustworthy guide for faith and practice. It is not only an inspiring and comforting devotional book, it is also instructive and practical. Our other-worldly approach to Christian principles often makes Christianity impractical in the day-to-day activities of life. People who have an inspiring devotional life which, they say, gives them strength to face the challenges of the day, may act in a very unchristian way in their business dealings. While they are 'inspired' by the Scriptures, they are not instructed by them. Biblical wisdom is down to earth, and very practical. It has a lot to say about our day-to-day life in a fallen world.

Wise and prudent people who want to know how to live in this world, would do well to use the Scriptures as their instruction book for all aspects of life. This includes family life, business life, social life, religious life, vocational life and all other areas.

## WISDOM ABOUT WHOM TO TRUST

In Proverbs 17:18 we are warned against trusting untrustworthy people:

> A man lacking in judgment strikes hands in
>     pledge
> and puts up security for his neighbour.

Similar advice is given in Proverbs 22:26–27:

> Do not be a man who strikes hands in pledge
>     or puts up security for debts;
> if you lack the means to pay,
>     your very bed will be snatched from under
>     you.

Striking hands in a pledge refers to shaking hands to seal a business matter. This idea of a covenant, as we said in the first chapter, was originally the significance of shaking hands. So we are told not to go into business deals with those we cannot trust. How many people have gone into deals, blinded to their dangers by the prospect of quick returns, and then had to face huge losses?

The second thing to avoid is standing as a guarantor for someone you don't know well enough to trust fully. It is good to help people in need. But it is foolish to trust strangers. When you act as a guarantor for someone, you say that you know this person well enough to be certain that he or she will keep his or her commitments. If you cannot be sure of that, then you must not stand up on behalf of that person.

Now we must add quickly that it is wrong to use the above passages as an excuse for not helping people in need. They simply warn us about the folly of trusting people we don't know. Elsewhere in the Bible we are urged to give freely to the poor. For example, Proverbs 19:17 says, 'He who is kind to the poor lends to the Lord.' Jesus said, 'Give to the one who asks you, and do not turn away from the one who wants to borrow from you' (Matthew 5:42). He went to the extent of urging us to lend to those who may not be able to pay us back: 'And if you lend to those from whom you expect repayment, what credit is that to you? Even "sinners" lend to "sinners", expecting to be paid in full' (Luke 6:34).

Proverbs 6:1–5 speaks with great urgency about what we should do if people we guarantee fail to fulfil their obligations. Verses 1 and 2 describe the situation such a person has got into:

My son if you have put up security
    for your neighbour,
if you have struck hands in a pledge for
    another,
    if you have been trapped by what you said,
ensnared by the words of your mouth . . .

The text goes on to say what we are to do in such a situation:

. . . then do this, my son, to free yourself,
    since you have fallen into your neighbour's
    hands:
Go and humble yourself;
    press your plea with your neighbour!

Releasing ourselves from these obligations may be humiliating as we plead with the creditor. But that is the price to pay for our folly.

Verses 4 and 5 stress the urgency of releasing ourselves from these financial obligations.

Allow no sleep to your eyes,
    no slumber to your eyelids.
Free yourself like a gazelle from the hand of
    the hunter,
    like a bird from the snare of the fowler.

Robert Alden explains the urgency thus: 'Don't let another day pass, don't wait until after the siesta. Set the record straight now and get out from under its obligation.'

Today many Christians live with the burden of unsettled financial dealings. These burdens take away their peace and fill them with anxiety. Such people have no freedom in their relationships because they often tend to hide the facts from their acquaintances. The result is that these unsettled financial matters hinder their testimony and thus greatly reduce their effectiveness as Christians.

Yet it is a mystery why an urgency to free themselves from these obligations is not found in the lives of many Christians. They will go on living as if nothing has happened. They will spend money on pleasures that are not essential for survival. While they remain in debt they say, 'I *must* have this', and 'I *must* have that'. But these things they 'must' have are not absolutely essential for a happy and healthy life. They will take a vacation in an expensive resort, or go to an expensive restaurant, or buy an expensive dress. When we say that we must have these non-essentials at the cost of settling our financial burdens, we show how far we are from the attitude of Christ. He did not even have a place to lay his head when he was on earth. This willingness to sacrifice the freedom from crippling financial obligations for the passing pleasures of materialism is a dangerous trend. Even nations continue with their affluent lifestyles while their national debt becomes bigger and bigger.

The Bible advocates a life free from the anxieties of unsettled financial obligations. It advocates urgency in settling these, because it views the resulting freedom as a great treasure. There is the very important principle of 'short accounts' which applies in many spheres of the Christian life and which applies here too. When we sin we should go to God at once, without delaying the confession. When we hurt someone we should apologize at once. Similarly when we have financial obligations we should deal with them at once. Many, on the other hand, duped by Satan, postpone settling these and give priority to passing pleasure. Satan has won a great victory in crippling God's children in this way and rendering them ineffective.

## SENSITIVITY TO EACH OTHER'S SCHEDULES

Seldom set foot in your neighbour's house –
too much of you, and he will hate you.
(Proverbs 25:17)

Kenneth Aitken's title for this verse is, 'Don't make a pest of yourself.' Proverbs has a lot to say about the price of friendship. But there is always a good reason for the way we sacrifice for others. Never do we sacrifice for the sake of sacrifice. So the price of friendship is always caused by a good purpose. One who makes a pest of himself does not have a good reason for imposing on another.

When we have a genuine need we may go to a very busy friend and get him or her to give up some precious time to help us. We should not be reluctant to do this. It is one of the necessary features of commitment. If we say that we should not disturb our 'busy friend' in our time of need, we are insinuating that our friend is not very committed to us. Our reluctance to go to him or her is a statement about how we rate our friendship. But there are some people who spend too long in another's presence without any good reason for doing so. These are selfish people.

Sometimes when my wife is having her devotions I feel like saying something to her. Most often it could wait until she has finished her appointment with her Lord, but there have been times when I haven't waited. Then I was acting in the way condemned in this passage: I was unnecessarily imposing on her.

The key to this verse is sensitivity and consideration. Friends should be concerned about the different areas in the lives of other people and act in a way that expresses sensitivity to them.

If my mother-in-law is at our home and she is talking to my wife when I come home from work, she leaves the room when I come in. This is not because she does not like me (!), but because this is the time I would like to be with my wife. Her concern for us makes her leave the room.


## SINFUL SEXUAL RELATIONSHIPS

Adultery is a sinful form of friendship and Proverbs has a lot to say about its lure and its dangers. There are vivid warnings to keep away from situations that could make one open to temptation:

> For the lips of an adulteress drip honey,
>     and her speech is smoother than oil;
> but in the end she is bitter as gall,
>     sharp as a double-edged sword.
> Her feet go down to death;
>     her steps lead straight to the grave.
>                           (Proverbs 5:3–5)

At first there is a great attraction to this relationship. But it drags one down to the way of death.

A most vivid description of how a person falls into sexual temptation is given in Proverbs 7. It does not seem that the young person mentioned here had planned to fall into this temptation. He was seduced. And that was possible because he was 'a youth who lacked judgment' (Proverbs 7:7). One evening, as he was walking down the street, 'out came a woman to meet him, dressed like a prostitute and with crafty intent' (verse 10). Verses 13–21 describe how, 'with persuasive words she led him astray; she seduced him with her smooth talk' (verse 21).

There was a powerful attraction in what she offered: 'Come, let us drink deep of love till morning; let us enjoy ourselves with love' (verse 18). The immediate satisfaction and thrill that come from sexual sin are responsible for its great appeal. This appeal is intensified in today's society where the motto, 'If it feels good, it's got to be right', is so popular. In such an environment, when faced with temptation, many find it very difficult to resist.

The young man in Proverbs seems undecided about how to respond to this seduction. But suddenly passion rules him and good sense ceases to influence him: 'All at once he followed her like an ox going to the slaughter, like a deer stepping into a noose' (verse 22). How many have been carried away by passion like this, doing things that they would not do in their right minds. But the young man was in the wrong place. He had 'entertained' the temptation for too long. Consequently he was powerless to resist.

This episode brings out the wisdom of Paul's advice to Timothy: 'Flee the evil desires of youth' (2 Timothy 2:22). We must not try to negotiate with sin. In certain situations it is best to leave the scene of temptation immediately, as Joseph did when seduced by Potiphar's wife at a time he was alone in the house with her (Genesis 39:12).

The section in Proverbs ends with a warning:

Now then, my sons, listen to me;
  pay attention to what I say.
Do not let your heart turn to her ways
  or stray into her paths.
Many are the victims she has brought
    down . . .

(Proverbs 7:24–26)

This type of warning is found over and over again
in Proverbs (2:10–11, 16–19; 5:1–23; 6:20–35;
9:13–18; 22:14; 23:26–28; 30:18–20). The fre-
quency of the occurrences of these warnings should
sober us. The point is that, because sexual passions
can be easily aroused and at such times it is difficult
to control oneself, wise people are doubly careful
in this area. Proverbs 30:18–20 says,

There are three things that are too amazing for
    me,
  four that I do not understand:
the way of an eagle in the sky,
  the way of a snake on a rock,
the way of a ship on the high seas,
  and the way of a man with a maiden.

This type of care is a key feature of the wisdom
which 'will save you also from the adulteress' (Proverbs 2:16). It was the young man's failure to be
careful that made him 'a youth who lacked
judgment'.
The heart of wisdom, however, is having the
Word of God close to us all the time.

My son, keep my words
  and store up my commands within you.
Keep my commands and you will live;

53

guard my teachings as the apple of your eye.
Bind them on your fingers;
    write them on the tablet of your heart.
(Proverbs 7:1–4)

These verses describe an intimate contact with and careful attitude to the Word. Our concern for it, in Kidner's words, is to be as sensitive as our care for the pupil (apple) of the eye. It is interesting that these four verses about our attitude to the Word are the prologue to the chapter we looked at about the seductress and the young man who lacked judgment. The idea is that one who conscientiously seeks to know and obey the will of God will be sensitive to the approach of temptation. This attitude is well described in a hymn of Charles Wesley:

I want a principle within
Of jealous godly fear,
A sensibility to sin,
A pain to feel it near.

I want the first approach to feel
Of pride or fond desire,
To catch the wandering of will,
And quench the kindling fire.

That I no more from thee may part,
No more thy goodness grieve,
The filial awe, the fleshly heart,
The tender conscience, give.

Quick as the apple of an eye,
O God, my conscience make;

And keep my soul when sin is nigh,
And keep it still awake.

To my knowledge homosexual relations are not
mentioned in Proverbs. But warnings about this
too are in order in today's society. What could be a
beautiful relationship between two people of the
same sex can be spoiled if a physical, sexual content
is permitted to invade that relationship.

## THE VULNERABILITY OF
FRIENDSHIP

The word *'allup* is the strongest possible word to
use for friendship. It has the idea of bosom companion. But it is used three times to describe the
vulnerability of friendship. The first time is in Proverbs 2:16–17 which speaks of 'the wayward wife
... who has left the partner (*'allup*) of her youth
and ignored the covenant she made before God'.
Here we are presented with the pain of a marriage
broken through the unfaithfulness of a partner.

The other two times the word *'allup* appears in
connection with the vulnerability of friendship are
in descriptions of the way loose talk can destroy a
friendship. In Proverbs 16:28 we read, 'A gossip
separates close friends', and then in chapter 17:9,
'Whoever repeats the matter [of an offence committed by a friend] separates close friends.'

These sobering proverbs remind us that there are
limitations to what we can hope for from friendships. They can fail us. And when that happens we
end up deeply hurt. Because of this some people
never cultivate close friendships, but that is not
biblical. Remember that even Jesus had to face the

pain of having his disciple Judas betray him. But he placed a high priority upon his relationship with his close friends, the disciples. This ought to comfort us and challenge our reluctance to cultivate close friendships.

## THE PRIMACY OF OUR RELATIONSHIP WITH GOD

But more importantly, the references to the vulnerability of friendship teach us that all human friendships are limited in their scope and reliability. Always our most important relationship must be with God. Those who jeopardize their relationship with God are sacrificing the eternal for the temporal. Even our spouses must never take a higher place than God.

Of course, this is in keeping with the teaching of Proverbs. Before launching into all the great words of wisdom, Proverbs first gives us the basis for all this wisdom. In chapter 1:7 we read,

> The fear of the Lord
> is the beginning of knowledge.

We must never read Proverbs without this perspective. It is a book of wisdom. Now some of the wisdom found in Proverbs is found in other religions also. But what makes it unique is that for children of God, all wisdom springs from our relationship with God. Proverbs 3:5–6 teaches the primacy of our relationship with God even more vividly:

> Trust in the Lord with all your heart
> and lean not on your own understanding;
> in all your ways acknowledge him,
> and he will make your paths straight.

Our relationship with God is basic.

However, putting God first does not hurt human friendships. It can only strengthen them. In fact, this perspective gives the foundation for a stable friendship. You see, if our stability comes from God and we expect total goodness from him alone, we will be secure people. Those whose security is in God will not try to grab it from other people. Insecure people who look to others for their primary source of security put a huge burden on them, because they expect so much from their friends or spouses. Friends and spouses are afraid of failing to live up to their expectations, and so are not free to enjoy the relationship. They always wonder, 'Now will he or she get upset with me?'

It is right to have expectations of people, but these must not be unrealistic. The trouble is that insecure people try to grab from fallible people things that they can get from God alone, such as absolute perfection and personal security.

Those who find their security in God can risk loving others. The love may be rejected, or the loved one may fail and disappointment may result. But the Christian has the strength to go on because the earthly relationship is not the most important thing in life. Some people don't want to risk loving because they are afraid that it might result in disappointment. As Christians, we know that, even if we are disappointed, the most important thing in life, our relationship with God, is not touched. Nothing can separate us from the love of Christ. So we can handle the battering that comes from the disappointments of earthly love.

But there is more to our relationship with God than security. The glory of the gospel is that our relationship with God is not some supra-spiritual reality which has no connection with the realities of life in a hostile and fallen world. We go to God through Jesus Christ. And Jesus is our brother and friend. Hebrews 2:17 puts this strikingly: 'For this reason he had to be made like his brothers in every way, in order that he might become a merciful and faithful high priest in service to God.' By becoming our brother, Jesus could be our high priest, that is, our mediator.

The writer of Hebrews goes on to make a further point about the brotherhood of Jesus in the next verse when he says, 'Because he himself suffered when he was tempted, he is able to help those who are being tempted.' Jesus *suffered* when he was tempted! He did not sail through temptation with consummate ease as we would have expected the Son of God to do. That suffering qualified him to be our brother, to identify with us.

When we go to God with our struggles he does not simply look at us with condescending benevolence and drop some 'sufficient grace' from heaven to give us strength to cope. Rather, because he knows the pain of it, not only does he give us strength to face up to it, he comes to us as a comforting friend. And how much we need a friend in times of trouble. It is such a source of comfort and release to be able to say, 'At least he understands!' When we weep, it is a comfort to know that Jesus also wept. When we are betrayed by our friends, it is a comfort to know that Jesus also was betrayed. When people in whom we have placed a lot of trust fail us, it is a comfort to know that, after three years of constant companionship and training, Peter denied Christ.

So if you are going into close friendships, be prepared to be hurt. Don't expect from them what you should be expecting from God alone. If you do, your hurt will damage you permanently. If your trust is in God, you will still be hurt, because God made you with the capacity to love. That capacity includes in it the vulnerability to personal hurt. But that hurt will drive you to God – to bask in his comfort; to lean on his love. In fact, the hurt will drive you closer to God. Your bitterness will be washed away along with the tears that you shed in the presence of God. You may continue to be sad, because the earthly conditions may not change, but you will not be broken or bitter. The most important thing about your life is still intact. You are loved of God. So amidst the pain, there is a brightness in you that love alone can give.

Have you ever been deeply hurt? A lover has disappointed you? A marriage that started with much promise has turned sour? A person in whom you invested much has betrayed you? Go to Jesus! He knew what it was to be betrayed by his close friends. But he will never betray you. Lean on his gentle breast. And weep away your bitterness as you release your burdens to him.

He will not only heal you; he will also draw you nearer to himself than you were before. Later, when you look back at the pain, there may still be sorrow, but there will not be bitterness. Bitterness by now has been replaced by the love of God in your heart. So you will be grateful to God: grateful for the way he healed you; grateful for the things he taught you through these experiences.

# CHAPTER FOUR

# UNSELFISH COMMITMENT

We are talking in this book of friends who stick closer to us than a brother (Proverbs 18:24). The word translated here as 'sticks' is the same word used of Ruth clinging to her mother-in-law, Naomi (Ruth 1:14). The basic idea is that of commitment. In this and the chapters that follow we will see how Proverbs and Ecclesiastes describe what this commitment is like.

## SELFISH RELATIONSHIPS

Commitment is a concept that has gone out of fashion in today's society. Why? Because most of our relationships today are purely selfish. The writer of Proverbs often speaks about selfish relationships. For example, in chapter 14:20 we read:

The poor are shunned even by their
　　neighbours,
　but the rich have many friends.

Chapter 19:4 says something very similar,

Wealth brings many friends,
　but a poor man's friend deserts him.

Both these verses condemn the insincerity of
people who befriend the rich because of what they
can get from them and neglect the poor because
they are of no use to them (or so they think).

This type of behaviour is not all that alien to us
today. Just look at the way a church usher wel-
comes a rich and influential person at the entrance
to a church, and then compare it with the way that
same usher greets a badly dressed and desperately
poor person. That may reveal to us how utilitarian
we are in our approach to people. Actually such
poor people rarely do enter our churches. They feel
so uncomfortable and unwelcome in an average
church that they don't usually like to come in. (I
believe this gives us a strong reason to dress simply
when we go to church. But this is another topic
altogether!)

Proverbs 19:6 says,

Many curry favour with a ruler,
　and everyone is the friend of a man who
　　gives gifts.

For a modern expression of this bias, go to an
International Christian Conference. There you will
see that people will often ignore the unknown dele-
gates and vacillate to the famous. Some go to the
extent of bringing gifts for these well-known

people, even though they may be the least needy. While talking to an 'unknown saint', they may suddenly break off in mid-sentence, and start talking to a famous Christian who has just appeared on the scene.

The rich, the generous and the powerful may have a lot of friends. We may be tempted even to envy the powerful because of this. But that is because we are so blinded by the lure of the immediate but shallow satisfaction that prominence may bring. Actually, we should feel sorry for the powerful people who have this type of friends, for it is so hard for them to find real friends. And if they fall from their positions of power, which is a common occurrence today, their 'friends' desert them.

How unlike the Christian model all this is. It is, of course, the marketing model of a lot of businesses who set apart significant sums of money to curry favour with influential people. But the Bible on the other hand presents God and his followers as having a particular eagerness to befriend and help needy people. In fact a key way to test someone's Christian character is to observe the way they treat insignificant people when they think no-one is watching them.

The principle that we glean from this is that many friendships in life are essentially selfish. Our commitment has been to the actual work a person can do for us, not to the person. That work may be giving us something from his or her wealth or power. Or it may be the work that the person does for the group that he or she belongs to. When the person leaves the group or expresses interest in doing so, then all the concern showed earlier is forgotten. The friendship remains as long as it is a help to us. This is the age of disposable relationships. Perhaps most friendships today are like that.

One of America's most respected analysts of social trends and public attitudes, Daniel Yankelowich, has written a book called *New Rules: Searching for Self-fulfillment in a World Turned Upside Down*. He shows that in Western society, where the aim of people is self-fulfilment, a new set of rules has developed that govern our actions. A lot of what he says is beginning to appear in developing nations also. One of these new rules is that lasting commitments are out. We remain committed to an organization or person, so long as we think it advantageous to us. When it is considered to be of no use to us, we drop it.

## WHEN WE LEAVE A GROUP

There may come a time when a person has to leave a group to which he or she has been committed. Perhaps there is no suitable place in the organization for a person with his or her abilities. Perhaps his or her vision can best be fulfilled elsewhere. Perhaps he or she is moving to a new area and needs to find a new church. At such a time, the Christian model would be to make the transition as helpful to the person as possible.

A lot of hurt has developed in people because of the way they have been dropped by groups they worked with when the group felt it no longer had a place for them. They had laboured so sacrificially in this group, now they are just dropped! The leaders of these groups were certainly not friends who stuck closer than brothers. In fact their style of friendship was closer to the style of selfish relationships we have just looked at.

When a daughter decides that it is time for her to leave home, the parents won't just drop their concern for her. They will do everything to help make the transition as smooth as possible. This example from family life is very appropriate as churches and Christian organizations are often described as families. Just as parents help their children, so leaders should try to find the best place for the person who has decided to leave their group.

The leaders could, for example, make use of contacts they may have, to help find a good job for this person. Leaders usually have such contacts. When a church member leaves the area, the church can do its best to commend this person to a church in his or her new area so that he or she could merge into that community swiftly and effectively.

If a person leaves an organization he or she is working with, in order to go for further studies, the leaders could try to raise some funds for his or her studies. Usually we fund only the studies of those who will work for us after their studies are over. But how about those who have served us faithfully and sacrificially for many years and now sense it is time to leave us? Do we give them only the gratuity which the government laws require? No. Our righteousness must exceed that of the scribes and pharisees. We may be called to help in some way to fund their education because of our gratitude and concern for them. After all, these are people whose welfare has been a God-given responsibility of the leaders of the organization.

If we adopt the attitude just described, the departure of a worker from a group could be done in a way that is honouring to the Lord. Then the person leaving would not harbour deep hurts that people who were so close to him or her do not seem to care. He or she does not have to apply for jobs in secret and then suddenly announce his or her departure – to the consternation of all. In situations like this, young believers are often the ones most hurt. What has happened to all the teaching they received about fellowship? What are they to think when the person who taught them these things acts in a way that contradicts everything and suddenly leaves?

Sometimes we may ask a person to leave the group for disciplinary reasons. That does not, however, eliminate our responsibility to show concern to the person. We may, for example, help a person who has to leave paid 'full-time' Christian service to find a job in a business establishment.

It may seem at first to be a costly thing for a group to be committed to people in the way described above. But such groups will be blessed with committed members. Commitment breeds commitment. And what a great blessing committed people are in an age where commitment has gone out of fashion.

## COVENANT LOVE AND DISCIPLINE

It is most significant that the great word *hesedh*, used in the Old Testament to describe God's covenant-keeping love for Israel, is used in Proverbs to describe friendship.

> What a man desires is unfailing love;
> better to be poor than a liar.
>
> (Proverbs 19:22)

The NIV translates *hesedh* as 'unfailing love'. The RSV and others translate it as 'loyalty'. The idea is that just as God remains faithful to his covenant with Israel whatever the situation may be, we must be faithful to our friends.

In the following chapters we will see some of the ways in which this loyalty manifests itself. Here we will look at one aspect of covenant-keeping loyalty that is usually not associated with contemporary understandings of loyalty.

The Old Testament covenants included stipulations, and, in the covenant-making rituals, blessings for keeping the covenant and curses for breaking it were often read. Old Testament history shows that God's type of loyalty to Israel did not condone her sinfulness. When Israel sinned, God judged her. But he did not give up on the Israelites. Similarly, when our friends sin and we get into trouble through that, we don't ignore their sin. We would back whatever just disciplining is meted out to the person, for,

> Stern discipline awaits him who leaves the path.
>
> (Proverbs 15:10)

Church discipline is another of those biblical practices which is so rarely seen in the church. I suppose that is to be expected in churches that seem to be dedicated to making people feel good. Discipline is unpleasant not only for those doing the disciplining, but also for those disciplined and the other members of the church.

Indeed the work of disciplining wrong-doers is one of the most unpleasant aspects of a leader's work. Often something in him says, 'Ignore the problem.' Sometimes other Christians take this ignoring of the problem as a sign of patience. That is why we hear statements like, 'He's such a saint. He will never scold anyone.' But that is not saintliness. That is an expression of our fallenness. It happens when we don't take sin as seriously as God does. We often prefer to have the nice feeling that comes from being accommodating of everybody. So we ignore sin when we should be disciplining it.

People who ignore discipline are often known to be nice people. But, as someone has said, 'Nice guys have no cutting edge.' No-one may dislike them, but they are unable to influence sinners significantly to walk along the path of holiness.

Today, we often see Christians taking one of three inadequate routes when confronted by the need to discipline. First, they avoid disciplining a very useful person because the cost is considered too much. Take the situation where a very talented musician commits a fairly serious indiscretion. This becomes known shortly before an important musical programme. If biblical discipline was carried out he should not appear in public. But without him the programme would be greatly hampered, for it is too late to find a replacement. So he appears on the programme. But by allowing him to appear in this way we violate the covenant relationship we have with the musician. Christian love includes the commitment to respond to wrong-doing with justice.

The second inadequate approach is to attack the

problem too late. This could happen if there is no regular opportunity for the supervisor to advise and rebuke those in his or her charge. Sometimes the supervisor might not know what is happening. Other times the supervisor is reluctant to advise and rebuke because it simply does not seem the appropriate thing to do with a person one is not very close to. But sometimes the problem grows and becomes very serious. If a disciplinary inquiry has to be conducted at that stage the result is a lot of heartache all round. Often what would have been dealt with at a much earlier stage with a few words of advice or rebuke is unnecessarily allowed to grow into a major crisis.

The third inadequate approach is to discipline the person and then forget about him or her because he or she cannot help any more in our programme. That too is unloving, for our commitment to each other is not primarily because of our talents. Though we may not use this particular person in our programme we can meet with him or her and spend time trying to restore him or her. Surely this is the time he or she needs that companionship most.

The only time we are justified in rejecting a person is after all approaches have been tried and the person concerned rejects all of it because he or she refuses to repent. Such a person's heart has been hardened. The best thing to do is to refuse to accept this person into fellowship as long as his or her heart is hard.

1 John 1:7 says that to have fellowship with one another we must first walk in the light. This does not mean we must all be perfect. The verse next talks of the person being cleansed from sin. Christians who have sinned badly can have fellowship with other Christians. In fact, they really need this fellowship

after they have fallen. But if the fellowship is going to be deep, they must first accept their sinfulness, that is, confess their sin. Then they will be walking in the light.

If they refuse to do this, we cannot ignore their refusal. We may be called upon to stop associating with them in the hope that the pain of rejection might jolt them into regarding their sin with more seriousness. Jesus said that if we have tried all this and a person still refuses to repent we must treat him or her as we would a pagan or a tax collector (Matthew 18:15–17). R. T. France, in his book *The Gospel According to Matthew*, comments on this passage that 'after all persuasion has failed, a cold shoulder may still bring him to his senses' (page 275). Paul handed over Hymenaeus and Alexander to Satan (that is, expelled them from the fellowship), so that they may be 'taught not to blaspheme' (1 Timothy 1:20).

This is the price of Christian friendship. It is so much easier to ignore the sin and continue the friendship. But if we do this, we are unfaithful to the person, and we act differently to the way God does with his covenant people.

## COMMITMENT TO PRAY

Before we end this section, it would be good to discuss an aspect of commitment which, to my knowledge, does not appear in Proverbs but is found often in the Old and New Testament. This is the commitment to pray for one another. While we have a general commitment to pray for a large number of people, we have a special commitment to pray for those who are particularly close to us.

Paul told Timothy, his special friend and spiritual child, '. . . night and day I constantly remember you in my prayers' (2 Timothy 1:3).

Prayer is like fuel to a Christian relationship. The most important tie in Christian friendship is our common union with Christ. Therefore it is essentially a spiritual fellowship. So when we talk to God about one another we are strengthening the ties we have with each other.

Praying is something we can do no matter how distant we are from a person. This is something that I find helps me to remain close to my family and colleagues as I travel. On my trips I cannot spend time talking with them, but I can pray for them daily. And I know they pray for me. Through this prayer for each other a spiritual closeness is maintained.

There is a word here for leaders. We have a special tie of friendship with those whose work we supervise. As their leaders we are their servants. The greatest service we can do for them is to pray for them as Paul did for Timothy. It is significant that the only mention in the gospels of Jesus talking about his own prayer life is when he told Peter that he had prayed for him (Luke 22:32). The longest prayer recorded in the gospels is Jesus' prayer in the Upper Room, the majority of which was his intercession for the disciples (John 17:6–19).

During the time Vedanayakam Azariah was Bishop of the Anglican Church in South India, the Christian church experienced a great revival and many Hindus were added to it. It has been said that one of the secrets of his effectiveness as a Bishop was his practice of praying daily for each of the pastors in his diocese.

The apostles in the early church asked that they be separated for prayer and the ministry of the Word (Acts 6:4). One aspect of the prayer mentioned here must have been praying for those they led. Like Moses did so many times, we are called to intercede on behalf of those we lead. We should regard prayer as a basic feature in the 'job description' of a Christian leader. The prophet Samuel regarded as a sin the failure to pray for the people whose spiritual leader he was. He told Israel, 'As for me, far be it from me that I should sin against the Lord by failing to pray for you' (1 Samuel 12:23).

Not only do we pray for others, we also ask others to pray for us. This is a way in which we affirm the tie that we have with others. In eight of his thirteen letters Paul asks his readers to pray for him.

In ten of Paul's letters he mentions praying for his readers. This suggests that it is good to tell our friends that we pray for them. It will certainly be an encouragement to them, especially when they are going through a difficult time. It will also deepen the tie between the one who prays and the one who is prayed for.

# CHAPTER FIVE

# COMMITMENT IN *T*IMES OF *T*ROUBLE

We have said that commitment is the key to Christian friendships. But commitment is also one of those words that has suffered from what we call the 'inflationary trend', where words are cheapened and lose their original meanings. The fact that a person claims to be committed to another does not necessarily mean that the commitment is real. It is when a person is in trouble that we can really know whether the commitment is genuine.

## THE UNFAITHFUL

In Proverbs 25:19 we read,

> Like a bad tooth or a lame foot
> is reliance on the unfaithful in times of
> trouble.

A person depends on his teeth and feet for eating

and walking, which are basic functions of life. A bad tooth and a lame foot are parts that are intended to be important but have become useless to the body. What the proverb is saying is that we may depend on someone for crucial help in a time of crisis only to find that this person fails us. The importance of commitment emerges in this verse too, in the word 'unfaithful'. A true friend is faithful.

One of the saddest instances of unfaithfulness in the Bible is described in 2 Timothy 4:16 where Paul says, 'At my first defence, no-one came to my support, but everyone deserted me.' One of history's greatest warriors was on trial for the gospel, and the Christians did not want to associate with him. It simply was not personally advantageous (according to earthly values) to be committed to Paul at that time.

Why do we forsake people when they are in trouble? Because it costs to love at such times. Sometimes the cost we seek to avoid is *the shame of associating with people who are down*. This is what Paul had to face when he went to his trial.

We see this type of unfaithfulness often in places of work today. Say, for example, the head of the division has suddenly started finding fault all the time with a particular friend of yours who has been a faithful and hard worker for many years. It has become apparent that to cut costs the management has decided to discontinue his services. So they are looking for ways to highlight his shortcomings. You see what is happening and realize that there is no guarantee that your place in the company is secure. It would be best to be in the good books of the management. So when the boss speaks ill of your friend unjustly, you agree, not because he is right, but because you don't want to jeopardize your own place in the company.

This type of behaviour is so common today that people accept it as the norm. Many have come to accept that selfishness of this sort is a necessary evil in our competitive society. Yet it is clearly condemned in the Scriptures. And so we must not only abstain from selfishness ourselves, but also we must condemn it faithfully. We need to work towards making people realize that it is a dirty and low down thing to forsake a friend for the sake of our own convenience.

Failing to help a friend is a 'sin of omission' and therefore may often get overlooked. It rarely appears in a typical catalogue of sins. But it is a very common sin and therefore needs to be addressed by us.

Perhaps the most usual reason given for not helping others in their hour of need is that *there is no time for it*. Here, the cost is the inconvenience of giving time. We may need to visit the person and spend time with him or her when he or she is depressed or facing a crisis. We may need to do some things to help if he or she is confined to bed or overloaded with work.

When a friend has a crisis, then it becomes an urgent problem for us. However busy we are, we should do something to help him or her. Usually the really busy people are the only ones who will have time. I once saw a sign that said: 'If you want something done, ask the busy people. They are the only ones who will have the time.' These people will find the time to help somehow. Such people will have a lasting influence for good in this world.

They have invested, at personal cost, in the lives of others, many of whom will have been permanently changed by their ministry and example.

There are a lot of very nice people in the world who never have that type of influence. Few speak ill of them. They have not harmed anyone. But the people they have helped are generally limited to their own family circle. They will not inconvenience themselves to get involved in the problems of others. They may be nice people, but they dishonour Christ. He told his followers, 'As the Father has sent me, I am sending you' (John 20:21). Christ's model of sacrificial service is now our model. We are people who give our lives for our friends like Christ did (John 15:12–13). To fail to do this is to dishonour Christ.

Indeed, it is often true that we don't have the time to help people in need. But the loving, busy people *make* the time at a cost to themselves. We somehow find time for the things we regard as our priorities. As Christians, the needs of our friends should be a priority. So we should make the time for them.

I realize that this type of lifestyle is not very popular today. This is partly because some Christians have been irresponsible in their service: they have neglected their families; they have ruined their health; they have done things that others could have done. And all this was in the name of service.

But there is a responsible way of doing costly service: the balanced life approach. Living the balanced life does not mean doing everything in moderation, though that is what it means to many people. Moderation is often an excuse for taking things easy. The balanced life for the Christian means being obedient in every area of life. So the person who helps is committed to finding time for his family also.

This type of balanced living may not always be easy. After an exhausting time of counselling a troubled friend you may not feel like talking to your spouse when you go home, even though you should. You may feel like going to bed or watching television to get some emotional release. Obedient Christians will make themselves talk to their spouses, even though they do not feel like it, because that is a part of their Christian responsibility.

I must add that if you obey in this way, God will give you the strength and sustain you. This is the miracle of God's faithfulness to the obedient. Paul says, 'I labour, struggling with all his energy, which so powerfully works in me' (Colossians 1:29). There is labour and struggle, but there is also God's energy which works powerfully in us. The experience of that energy makes life exciting and meaningful. Those who 'play it safe' by living for themselves will never know the excitement of having the power of God working through them.

I believe that to many of us the cross we are called to bear is the balanced life. We often see people who are so involved in ministry that they neglect their family life. Or we see people who are so dedicated to their families that they neglect their responsibility to be active in some ministry. Both these are easy ways out. The difficult path to travel is that of trying to do both. This is the way of balance, the way of the cross.

The same principle applies to the need for rest. If we lose a lot of sleep one night because we had to help a person who was in need, then we have the responsibility to make up the much-needed rest somehow. People, of course, point out that you can never recover lost sleep. True, but as we said there is a price to pay for the life of service. Here we labour and toil (Colossians 1:29). We have a whole eternity to rest from our labours (Revelation 14:13).

Of course, when you hear that someone is in trouble, that does not mean that you are the only person who can help. The leader who gets too much ego gratification from his ministry falls in to this trap. Such people can drive themselves to complete exhaustion by allowing their ministries to become too dependent on themselves. Sometimes when we hear that someone is in need all we may have to do is make sure that somebody helps that person. We should be motivated by a concern for that person's welfare and should be happy if that person is helped even though we may not be the helper.

We must not let the abuses of the principle of sacrificial service deter us from involvement in it. This is an age that has a lot of slogans about friendship. The shops carry different kinds of cards on friendship that can be mailed to our friends. We hear statements like 'I love you' more often than before. In some circles hugging as a sign of friendship has become very popular. But all these things have got very cheap because they are not accompanied by costly commitment.

## FOR BETTER, FOR WORSE

The idea of the faithfulness of friendship being

shown when there is trouble is put forward in Proverbs 17:17. It says,

A friend loves at all times,
    and a brother is born for adversity.

The statement, 'a friend loves at all times', is another way of saying, '. . . for better, for worse; for richer, for poorer; in sickness, and in health; till death us do part'. Christian friendships are not 'fair weather' friendships. This principle applies absolutely to marriage, but it does apply to other friendships too, which is the case in this passage.

Let us apply this principle to the marriage relationship which is the most important of all friendships. Marriage has been under fire a lot in the West recently. One of the responses to this has been to major on the romance of marriage. We have books on how to bring the spark back into the relationship. There is a lot of emphasis on the fact that love is an enjoyable thing which, of course, is true. Many hints are given on how couples can 'enjoy' their relationship.

All this emphasis on the romance of marriage is very good. But it would be useless without commitment. Romance without the security of commitment produces a hollow enjoyment. When troubles come, romance vanishes from these relationships. When a child or one partner gets very sick there may be no possibility for these so-called romantic activities. You can't, for example, go on a vacation when someone is seriously sick. At such times the relationship always faces special strains, but if it is too dependent on romance the strain becomes much more serious. Sometimes the relationship becomes such a burden that it is dropped.

78

I have often wondered whether this has something to do with the number of divorces I have heard of that took place after a family crisis. For example I know of parents who divorce after enduring a long struggle because of the sickness of a child.

Commitment gives a security upon which you can build romance. Christian love does have a romance to it, but because it springs from commitment it is so much more enjoyable and deeply satisfying. You don't have doubts at the back of your mind whether this will last or not. With such doubts you cannot fully love a person or fully enjoy the love relationship. With commitment there is a mixture of security and freedom which makes the romance truly enjoyable.

Does the principle of sticking to relationships still apply when serious problems arise with incompatibility?

Incompatibility is a very popular word today. I believe that it is a symptom of this age's devotion to self-fulfilment. When self-fulfilment is defined in such a way as to preclude personal suffering, then incompatibility becomes grounds for divorce. The divorce epidemic in turn is a symptom of our society's inability to face suffering.

Christian commitment in marriage comes out of the belief that when the marriage vow to be faithful to the end was taken, being faithful to one's spouse became God's will for that person. That commitment gives us the strength to face up to the problem and work on a solution to it. If both the people are believers this becomes much easier. But even then, given our weaknesses, it will not always be easy. There will be struggle, there will be pain. But the commitment eliminates the option of splitting up.

Many couples have found that, after many stormy and painful years, finally God's grace won through and a joyous relationship emerged.

Other couples have not seen such resolution, perhaps because one partner was particularly difficult and inflexible. Then the other partner chose the path of suffering and refused to give up trying for a resolution. He or she had a whole eternity to enjoy the rewards of faithfulness in heaven. But even on earth we often find that this person was blessed by the children who were grateful for his or her faithfulness.

This way of thinking sounds strange today, because even many Christians have swallowed the approach to life that puts immediate fulfilment of aspirations above eternal principles. Biblical Christianity says commitments are worth sticking to even if that involves suffering.

For the Christian suffering is a normal part of life. In fact, if we are to enjoy a truly deep relationship with Jesus we *must* suffer. He was a suffering servant and, if we want to be like him, we also must suffer. That is why Paul desired the fellowship of sharing in Christ's suffering (Philippians 3:10). There is a depth of oneness with Christ that comes only through suffering. We may have pain that is difficult to bear, but in the midst of the pain we know a nearness to Christ that fulfils us. Though in pain, we are filled with a fullness that leaves us ultimately more complete than the restless pleasure-seekers who don't know the meaning of commitment. For the Christian, suffering is purposeful, so we will not compromise our principles in order to avoid suffering.

The attempt to have pleasure without commitment has doomed people to shallow emptiness. They may have their entertainment, their vacations, their 'precious independence'. But they are doomed to unfulfilment. They have tried to construct for themselves an unreal world – a world without pain and suffering. Those who accept suffering as a necessary part of life are not surprised when it comes. They won't be filled with the disillusionment that many have when they experience hardship. This disillusionment is what makes suffering so unbearable to many.

I do not want to increase the guilt and pain you feel if you are divorced. That is a step that has been taken. God can heal and start a new life for you. If you have confessed any sin on your part that may have contributed to the divorce and have handed yourself over to God for his care and direction, he will surely help you start a new chapter in your life, which is bright with the possibilities of grace. You may face the pain of loneliness and the regret over the past, but God will compensate with his presence and his direction that will enable you to experience the 'full life' that Christ alone can give (John 10:10).

My desire is to encourage all who are suffering or will face suffering because of commitments they have made. God may be calling you to endure pain and through that show the world that, co-existing with pain, there are deeper springs of fulfilment.

In Proverbs 17:17 we read also that 'a brother is born for adversity'. Derek Kidner has this to say: 'In trouble you see what family ties are, and you also see who are your friends.' Again the point is made that the best time to test friendship is when there are problems. Actually, one's behaviour when there is a problem is one of the best times to test not only friendship but also a person's character as well.

## SELF-FULFILMENT THROUGH FRIENDSHIP

Friendship and trouble are the subject of Proverbs 27:10 also:

> Do not forsake your friend and the friend of
>     your father,
>   and do not go to your brother's house when
>     disaster strikes you –
> better a neighbour nearby than a brother far
>     away.

The first part of this verse is a plea to keep up our friendships. The second part tells us what to do when we have an urgent need. We won't have the time to go in search of family members who live far away. So it is good to have friends nearby. They will help us when we are in trouble.

This reminds us again that commitment in friendship is not just an obligation which we must dutifully perform. Friendship is a help to us. Some seeking self-fulfilment may reject deep commitments because they see them as an unhelpful waste of time and energy. But all the so-called sacrifices of Christianity yield results that are beneficial to us. Jesus said that one who loses his life for the sake of the gospel will end up finding it. This principle applies to the cost of friendship too.

The irony is that those who give up commitment for the sake of self-fulfilment are not the ones who truly find fulfilment. It is the obedient Christian who is really self-fulfilled. It is typical of the deception of Satan to lead people away from the truth in search of something that only the truth can give them. Thus you find that people who can't be bothered with deep ties are lonely and unhappy. This is seen particularly when they are old or in trouble.

Now more than ever before, Christians should be reflecting on the truth given in the hymn that says, 'Make me a captive, Lord, and then I shall be free.' Commitment may seem to restrict us, but it is the only way to freedom.

# CHAPTER SIX

# WISDOM THROUGH FRIENDS

We ended the last chapter by stating that there are many blessings that we enjoy from friendship (many of them mentioned in Proverbs). The particular blessing we looked at was that of help in times of need. In this chapter we will look at the blessing of increased wisdom that comes to us through friends.

## ADVICE REGARDING OUR PLANS

The book of Proverbs often mentions the need to seek advice when making plans. In chapter 15:22 we read,

> Plans fail for lack of counsel,
>   but with many advisors they succeed.

This principle is applied to warfare in Proverbs 20:18:

Make plans by seeking advice;
    if you wage war, obtain guidance.

(See also Proverbs 11:14.) This principle can be applied to many different areas of our lives. If you are in some sort of ministry, it may apply to a strategy for ministry that you are about to adopt. It could be taken to apply to plans we have to expand our work, or to add on something to our house. It could also apply to that all-important decision we make regarding our partner in life. It could apply to the way we respond to people we have to deal with in some way.

I can think of at least two reasons why we need advice regarding our plans. Firstly, we often have an emotional attachment to our own plans which may blind us from seeing some of the pitfalls. This is 'our brainchild', the product of our creative efforts, so we fail to see the weak points because we are excited about the strong points. Secondly, the selfishness, from which none of us are totally free, could influence us to act in ways unbecoming of holy people. We may not realize that our action was motivated by selfishness until someone points it out to us.

We will begin by looking at an example of how our *emotions* can adversely affect our decisions. A young man is consumed by his attraction to a young lady. He believes it is true love, and becomes convinced this is the person he is going to marry. He talks to the girl about marriage. She accepts his proposal. After all this has been done they announce it to friends and relatives. A perceptive friend who is not blinded by the emotional force of attraction to the girl sees some real problems that could be expected if these two got married. But at this stage it seems to be too late to advise the person. And after the first glow of marriage fades they realize how mismatched they are. For the rest of their lives they regret the decision they took to get married to each other.

A similar thing happens when a person chooses a new job. The prospective employer 'promises him the skies' and he or she is blinded by the attractiveness of this job. Someone who can look at it more objectively may see problems which the person cannot see.

Why is it that people who know very well the value of advice, ignore it when making some of the most important decisions of their lives? Some people have an idea that a truly romantic courtship must not involve down-to-earth conversations with friends about the suitability of this tie. Some regard such recourse to friends as a violation of their independence. With the growth of individualism in our age this is becoming an increasingly common reason for neglecting advice in decision making. Others are so determined to follow their instincts, alas blinded by the force of this attraction, that they do not want to hear a negative word about it. This is an area where we must recognize our fallibility and look for advice from trusted friends.

In recent years we have seen many clergy divorces. Often a main cause for the divorce is that the spouse was not willing to adopt the lifestyle needed of a clergy spouse. It soon becomes clear that they should never have got married. But swept away by love, as they were, they ignored their differences and 'took the plunge'. We should not only blame the spouse, which is what is commonly done today. The minister was unfair to expect the spouse to adopt a lifestyle which he or she was not willing to adopt. They simply were not suited for each other.

I once asked an American clergyman whether an average ministerial candidate or minister gets any input from anyone in the ministerial community about the choice of his or her spouse. He said that there was no structure to facilitate such input. I thought that this was scandalous! What is the use of all this talk of community if the community cannot help its ministers when they make the most important decisions in their lives? My clergyman friend even went on to say that people prefer not to talk about their personal lives at ministerial meetings as that could jeopardize their progress in the ecclesiastical status ladder.

I must hasten to add that there *is* hope for a mismatched couple. God *can* change situations as his grace acts upon people and situations and brings healing. There are no irreconcilable differences if we open ourselves to God. The commitment people have to each other and the openness to God's moulding can lead to the path of healing. Of course, given our human weaknesses, that may be a long and painful path. And, as we said in the last chapter, many are not willing to traverse that path. The price of healing seems to be too much to bear. The time for healing seems to be too long to wait.

This then is an area where our emotions can deceive us. Now let us look at the area of personal relationships where *selfishness* can also cause us to make wrong decisions. Some of our acquaintances affirm our egos. They hang on to our every word.

They frequently compliment us, and we are comfortable in their presence. Others don't affirm us in this way. Perhaps they are not attracted to our way of doing things. Their personality may be such that they do not relate to people in a warm way in public. Perhaps they were very friendly with our predecessor and are disappointed that he or she was moved. So they will take some time to accept us. All of these things do not mean the second group are bad people. But their reaction to us is a blow to our pride.

We can be inaccurate in our judgments with both these groups of people because we are influenced by the way they affect our egos. I once heard the late Sri Lankan churchman, D. T. Niles, say that we generally categorize people into two groups. We regard the people we like as good and the others as bad. When the 'good' people do something wrong we find excuses for it. When the 'bad' people do something right we look for ulterior motives.

We can act in this way with people who affirm our egos, whom we place in the 'good' category, and those who do not affirm our egos, whom we place in the 'bad' category. So we can favour the 'good' people and be prejudiced against the 'bad' people. Team members will help us avoid these errors in judgment. They will see that decisions which have been influenced, often subconsciously, by our selfishness are wrong and they help us correct them.

Let me share two specific areas where I have often seen errors of the type mentioned above take place. I have found, mostly too late, that a person may relate in one way to his leaders and in a very different way to his peers and 'subordinates'. He may be very respectful and kind to his leaders but treat his peers and subordinates with disdain. I have also found, again often too late, that we are sometimes inaccurate in our judgments about people whom we disciple. These are people whom we regard as our spiritual children. We tend to overlook their weaknesses and too readily accept their explanations of errors they have made. Because of our ambitions for them, we like to see them make progress. So we may promote them to positions they are not suited for. We think they are suited for the jobs. But like most parents we are not very objective in our opinions about the abilities of our 'children'.

This is why, when taking disciplinary decisions and those related to promotions and other appointments, it is so important to get the advice of others who will be frank with us. Team members can help us to be more accurate in our judgments about such people.

## ADVICE REGARDING OUR BEHAVIOUR

Proverbs 12:15 says,

> The way of a fool seems right to him,
> but a wise man listens to advice.

The thrust of this verse is that we must not be too confident about the rightness of our motives and actions. Our friends may see some things that we may not see. Let me describe some examples of this.

Christians often get emotionally entangled with

members of the opposite sex without realizing that it is happening. Sometimes it is with a person with whom one works closely. Or it may be with someone to whom one gives a lift daily to work. It may be a person one is counselling. Whilst it might feel good to be able to help this person, through the prolonged contact an unhealthy emotional tie is developing. Things are said that should be spoken only to one's spouse.

Yet these relationships are regarded most often as 'just another Christian friendship'. Our minds have a way of deluding us like that. A Methodist Bishop in America has said that the history of the church has a long list of ministers who fell into sexual sin, thinking that they were the exception to the rule. They say that though others have got into trouble through relationships like this, this one is different. Suddenly it has gone too far. Good people have been hurt and become the subject of scandalous stories. God is dishonoured and effective ministries are ruined.

Even though we may delude ourselves into thinking that nothing harmful is happening, our friends may see its harm. They may notice that something more than a normal friendship is developing. It may be the way the eyes of the two people meet. It may be the amount of time they spend together. Or it may simply be the way they talk to each other. An observant person will sense that the relationship is going too far. The friend's words of warning could open his or her eyes to see the real situation and save him or her from so many woes.

Sadly, however, some people see these things happening and do nothing about it because they think it is none of their business. Even worse is the common practice, when people see or hear about such things, of telling others about it – gossiping – without talking to the person concerned. This is selfish thinking and alien to the Christian model of concern for the welfare of others.

The ones being advised may resent the type of involvement in their affairs which we are advocating. Leaders especially, find it difficult to take advice in this way. They have got so used to giving advice that they are unaccustomed to being on the receiving end. A survey of medical doctors recently revealed that preachers were among the hardest people to treat. They seem to think that they know everything and that makes it difficult for doctors to get them to follow their advice! Let us discipline ourselves into taking the advice of others seriously. We need others to show us when we are headed in the wrong direction.

## BECOMING WISE PEOPLE

Proverbs 19:20 says,

> Listen to advice and accept instruction,
> and in the end you will be wise.

Robert Alden says that this 'might be called the key verse of the book because it neatly summarizes what Proverbs is all about'. This verse is talking about a process. It is 'in the end' that the person becomes wise. We are not born wise. There are no short cuts to wisdom. Wisdom comes as the reward of applying oneself to knowledge.

Sometimes we are filled with admiration for a good writer. We observe how just the right words seem to flow from her pen. The free and easy-to-read style suggests that she has not laboured long and hard with communication. But if you were to ask this writer what made her so good, she would invariably recount the struggle to use just the right word, just the right phrase, especially in the early years. The dynamic style is the end product of a process that included hard work and patient revising and re-revising. Those early years of struggle helped stamp a dynamic writing style into her being.

It is like that with wisdom. It is not always easy to accept advice. But those who conscientiously submit themselves to the discipline of being advised by others will in the end be wise people. And what a wonderful quality that is to have! It is worth all the humiliation of being a learner when others confidently paraded themselves as experts. The 'experts' remained where they were. They did not think that they needed to learn. The humble learner, on the other hand, did not look too confident in the crowd. But his commitment to learning helped him to keep climbing so that at the end, he had reached heights that the other 'confident' people could never hope to reach.

## BEYOND RECEIVING ADVICE?

There can come a time when a person thinks that he or she is so knowledgeable, that he or she does not need advice anymore. To this person Proverbs 19:27 says,

> Stop listening to instruction, my son,
> and you will stray from the words of
> knowledge.

Derek Kidner titles this proverb 'Trifling with

truth'. The person has become careless, perhaps due to over-confidence.

This type of carelessness can hit us after we have achieved some success. People say, 'You were great.' And we believe them. But it is not true. Our preaching or our performance at our job or on the playing field may have been great. But there's more to life than preaching or one's job or the playing field. Life involves a lot of things like family life, thought life, devotional life and study life. Often we think that because we have done well in one area we are good in every area of life. But that is not true.

Because of our sense of achievement we can become careless and begin to stray from God's will. Our success contributes to the muffling of the questionings of our actions by the Spirit through our consciences. Because we have climbed so high there is no-one to challenge our actions and to feed our souls with spiritual food. Some 'top' leaders have no-one that they are spiritually accountable to. They have Boards to guide them on making policy decisions. They may have consultants who advise them on technical matters. But they have no-one to advise them in their day-to-day work.

True friends have a way of deflating the false bubble of success which we may have around us. They know us too well to put us up on a pedestal. They know our weaknesses which are often not seen in public. They help us come down to reality and realize that we are just ordinary people. But sometimes the fall is quite painful.

Here is a man who has just delivered a brilliant speech to a prestigious gathering. Many people praise him after the speech and by talking to them, he is late leaving for home. His wife had asked him to get some food for the family on the way back from the meeting. But, basking in the glow of praise, he forgot all about the food. Because he is so late home, the children are hungry, very restless and hence a strain on their mother's nerves. She meets her husband at the door and inquires first not about the speech but about the food.

He is jolted back to reality. His success as an orator does not make him immune to failure as a husband and father. He could snap back at her, saying the 'great work' of speaking to 1,000 people caused him to forget the 'little family chore'. But in God's sight greatness is not determined by the size of the audience! Parenting is also great work.

Is this why so many marriages are ruined after one spouse achieves some big success? Say it is the husband who has succeeded. This was what the wife had longed for. She dreamed of the day when her husband would be rich and famous. Now that dream has been fulfilled. But she cannot recognize the new person who emerged. He has started to live in the unreal world of success and fame.

People who are a success in public life must have close friends who will help them avoid the perils of success. If they are married their spouses are the best people to bring them down to earth. This will help them to avoid the moral failures that have sadly marred the lives of so many Christian leaders recently.

# CHAPTER SEVEN

# THE WOUNDS OF A FRIEND

Giving advice, as we saw in the last chapter, is not always a pleasant task. In fact Proverbs describes part of the role of a friend as that of wounding. This is so important that we will devote a whole chapter to it.

## WOUNDS VERSUS FLATTERY

Proverbs 27:5–6 says,

Better is open rebuke
than hidden love.
Wounds from a friend can be trusted,
but an enemy multiplies kisses.

Friends must wound us sometimes because they love us. This happens when they observe our weaknesses and errors. They have the responsibility to rebuke us. But wounds hurt and we are so afraid of pain that we sometimes prefer the kisses of an enemy. There is a charge here to consider the source of a statement and sometimes let that over-ride our immediate feelings about the statement. That is, if a friend has wounded us then we should not immediately dismiss the wounding as an unkind act. It may be a blessing in disguise.

But being honest is sometimes very painful and risky for the one doing the wounding. That is why chapter 27:6 describes it as 'wounds from a friend'. For a time we will really suffer from the con-sequences of doing it. We would appear to be unkind and unappreciative, perhaps judgmental and even jealous. But in the long run, it will be seen to have been worthwhile. Proverbs 28:23 says,

> He who rebukes a man will *in the end* gain
>     more favour.

When we realize that we were wrong and the friend who rebuked us was right, then if we have any integrity, we will express our gratitude to the rebuker.

I have a colleague, Tony, who is well known for his frankness. But he is also known for his faithful-ness to his friends, and many people go to him for counsel. Because of his non-traditional approach to life, many so-called 'way out' youths are not hesit-ant to befriend him. But because of his frankness he has infuriated many. He is not the type of person that everyone calls a 'nice guy'. Yet it is significant that when someone whom he has angered is in trouble or realizes that he or she was wrong after all, Tony is the first one that person goes to for help. Then he or she appreciates the fact that he had been honest with them.

I must hasten to add that there is a time and a

place for rebuking. Rebuking is not simply a thing that we do automatically with no consideration for how it will affect the one rebuked. Sometimes a valid rebuke can do more harm than good if it is done at the wrong time and place. Generally I try to avoid rebuking a person publicly. However, if the person's error has had a deep impact upon others we may have to rebuke him or her in public. Paul told Timothy that elders who sin 'are to be rebuked publicly, so that the others may take warning' (1 Timothy 5:20). However, usually we do not need to humiliate a person unnecessarily by rebuking him or her in public.

I have learned also that it may be good to wait for a time after someone has finished an emotionally draining activity, before we criticize it. For many people preaching is very tiring emotionally. Most preachers are encouraged by compliments that are given to them after a sermon. If the person has not done well and it would be of help to him or her to hear where he or she has failed, it may be better to wait until the emotional exhaustion from the event has died down. Otherwise he or she could over-react to the 'wound' by becoming discouraged, being too tired emotionally at this time to take the blow. But we do not need to offer compliments, which would be lying. We can simply keep quiet and wait for a more opportune moment.

However, sometimes we may need to point out a shortcoming at a time which isn't what we would term ideal, so that the person may be saved from making the mistake again. This happened to me at one of our English language Youth for Christ evangelistic camps. These camps are a real challenge to me as I have to battle to win the attention of

Westernized young people, many of whom know very little of Christianity and are not very interested in religious matters. As most of my ministry is with young people who are culturally more Eastern, I was particularly nervous as I spoke to this group.

I was giving a two-part series on the life of Christ. About half an hour before the second talk, Tony, my colleague of whom I spoke earlier, came into the dormitory where I was nervously doing my last minute preparations. A short while before he had met with the youth leaders at the camp for their daily evaluation session. He brought me the news that my first talk had gone over the heads of some of the youngsters.

It may not have seemed appropriate to say this to me half an hour before I went to speak. But it served to alert me to the need to do some fresh thinking on how to communicate more simply. I decided to discard my elaborate notes and hastily worked out a modified outline using the material in those notes. I added some new illustrations. Then I pleaded for help from God and rushed to the meeting hall. The report I received of that second talk was that I had communicated much better. How grateful I was to Tony that he was bold enough to tell me about the response to my first talk, even though the time seemed inappropriate. It takes commitment to do such things.

How do we know when to tell a person about his or her faults and when not to? That is a decision we have to make after weighing the pros and cons of the different options before us. The lesson that emerges from what I have just said is that we must approach our conversations with a serious resolve to please God and help our friend. It is a serious thing to wound a friend, but we may have to do that for his or her own good and for the glory of God. Someone who takes his or her relationships lightly will abstain from wounding because he or she does not want to face the consequences of that action. Or such a person will say simply what comes to mind without making sure that what he or she is going to say is correct and whether it is the best time to say it.

In contemporary society people are used to taking matters lightly that do not relate to their self-fulfilment. It is too troublesome to be worrying too much about other people. So they take a careless approach to their relationships. The only thing they take seriously is selfishness! These people will save themselves a lot of trouble, for wounding a friend is hard both on the wounder and the wounded. But they have been blinded from seeing that this way of self-denial for the sake of others, which is the way of the cross, is the only means to a deeply satisfying and liberated life. Because they don't pay the price of friendship, they don't experience the joys of friendship.

Proverbs 27:6 also says that 'an enemy multiplies kisses'. We may call these 'unkind kisses'. In this verse we have 'kind wounding' contrasted with unkind kissing. Perhaps the commonest form of this unkind kissing is flattery. And, as we saw, the commonest form of kind wounding is the rebuke. These two are found together in chapter 28:23 which says, 'He who rebukes a man will in the end gain more favour than he who has a flattering tongue.'

Flattery is a very dangerous thing. But it has

become so common today that we do not think much of its consequences. In chapter 29:5 we read,

Whoever flatters his neighbour
is spreading a net for his feet.

Flattery is described here as 'a net for his feet'. That is, it is like a trap that we can fall into. It makes us feel so good. But we may be feeling good about something that is wrong or needs to be changed. This is why flattery is so unkind. When we could be helping people we are harming them. It would be better to have not said anything.

## WOUNDS THAT INCREASE UNDERSTANDING

Rebuke and correction, which, as we have seen, sometimes come as wounds, help us to become wise people:

He who listens to a life-giving rebuke
will be at home among the wise.
He who ignores discipline despises himself,
but whoever heeds correction gains
understanding.

(Proverbs 15:31–32)

Christians who take their walk with God seriously, will soon realize that one of the most precious treasures in this world is wisdom. Our great desire in life is to do God's will. But it is not always clear what God's will is. There are so many decisions to make, so many voices crying for our attention, so many challenges before us, so many problems to solve. We are confronted all the time with questions like, what should I commit myself to? Whom should I support with my prayers, gifts and time? How can I stop this person from exploiting me? How do I know whether this 'opening' is a trap of Satan or an opportunity provided by God? What advice can I give this person who has come to me for help? How should I respond to this neighbour whose behaviour is taxing my patience so much? How can I motivate this discouraged colleague?

These are all challenges that call for wisdom. No wonder Proverbs has so much to say about the value of wisdom. Let me simply quote here one of the passages of Proverbs that exult over the value of wisdom.

Blessed is the man who finds wisdom,
    the man who gains understanding,
for she is more profitable than silver
    and yields better returns than gold.
She is more precious than rubies,
    nothing you desire can compare with her.
Long life is in her right hand;
    in her left hand are riches and honour.
Her ways are pleasant ways,
    and all her paths are peace.
She is a tree of life to those who embrace her;
    those who lay hold of her will be blessed.
                  (Proverbs 3:13–18)

If wisdom is such a valuable thing, we should be willing to pay a big price to procure it. Proverbs 15:31–32 tells us that often the price is the wounds or rebukes of a friend. We should be deeply grateful to a friend who rebuked us and through that helped to increase our understanding. It was painful at the time, just as it was painful for an Olympic gold medallist when his coach sent him through a rigorous training schedule before the Olympic games. With the gold medal in his possession, he would be glowing with praise for his coach. A wise person would realize that wisdom is of more importance for living than a gold medal. So we should be very grateful to the friends who are faithful in rebuking us. The fool has no such gratitude, for folly has blinded him or her from seeing the value of wisdom. It is these fools who are the topic of our next discussion.

## STUPID PEOPLE

If the rebukes of friends do so much good to us, then it is not surprising that Proverbs has some strong words to say about those who dislike being rebuked.

Whoever loves discipline loves knowledge,
but he who hates correction is stupid.
(Proverbs 12:1)

Stupid is a strong word! But that's what the NIV and RSV use here. Obviously it is intended to have a strong effect on the reader. Such is needed because we often try to avoid the pain of correction. We like to be saved from the embarrassment of looking stupid when our error comes to light. But here we are told it is actually this type of understanding of stupidity that is stupid.

One reason why such thinking is stupid is explained in Proverbs 13:18:

He who ignores discipline comes to poverty
and shame,
but whoever heeds correction is honoured.

One who does not take advice seriously will persist in his or her errors. These will lead to his or her downfall. I'm sure you have seen some bright people with tremendous potential lose their effectiveness because they did not heed advice.

Let's take an example. An evangelist decides that he wants to set up a hospital as part of his ministry. He believes the hospital will pay for itself through fees charged when it is in operation. But the experts tell him that there are sufficient hospital beds in the region and therefore he will have difficulty in keeping the new hospital going. They advise him against the project. He goes against their advice and builds the hospital. After a few years it becomes a heavy drain on his ministry, and he has to spend a lot of time and energy raising money to keep it going. He is detracted from his primary calling to be an evangelist. He did not listen to advice and was saddled with a heavy burden.

We need visionaries in the kingdom. But without advisors they could make big mistakes. With the help of advisors their visions will take practical, workable forms. The practical people may modify the plans here and there. But the result is that they become much better than the ones originally dreamed up by the visionaries. As they are put into operation and achieve so much good for the kingdom, the visionaries, who allowed their plans to be moderated by the practical people, are 'honoured' for their achievements (Proverbs 13:18).

The end product of heeding correction is honour. Billy Graham recounts how a senior Christian leader gave him some advice early on in his ministry after he had preached an evangelistic sermon. He told him that whenever he preaches an evangelistic message he should proclaim the cross of Christ. That ingredient of the gospel had been missing in the message he had just given. It is not easy for a preacher to accept such correction soon after preaching. But Graham took this advice and since then has faithfully preached the message of the cross for so many decades. And God has honoured his preaching.

There are other sobering verses in Proverbs that talk of the severe consequences of not heeding correction. They don't need much comment: their vivid language is comment enough.

> He who hates correction will die.
>
> (Proverbs 15:10)

> A man who remains stiff-necked after many
>     rebukes
>   will suddenly be destroyed – without
>     remedy.
>
> (Proverbs 29:1)


## TEACHABLE PEOPLE

If hating correction is stupidity, then the willingness to learn from others is the key to wisdom. It is therefore not surprising that Proverbs presents teachability as a high virtue:

> Apply your heart to instruction
>   and your ears to words of knowledge.
>
> (Proverbs 23:12)

This verse tells us to be eager to learn. The emphasis is placed on the more unpleasant aspect of teachability in chapter 17:10, the openness to be rebuked:

> A rebuke impresses a man of discernment
> more than a hundred lashes a fool.

(See also chapter 13:1.)

Some people are not very teachable because they try to project an image that they are mature or learned. They build a wall around themselves and their minds are difficult to penetrate especially when it comes to talking about their faults. The Bible on the other hand has much to say about the value of soft hearts that can be easily penetrated by God's Spirit and by fellow Christians who are the agents of the Spirit. This openness to penetration by the Spirit is the essence of teachability. Robert Alden's comment on Proverbs 17:10 is worth quoting here: 'People who are wise are also sensitive; their consciences are tender and their wills are pliant.'

This softness is one of the keys to holiness and is itself the mark of a true work of the Spirit in a person's life. This will be a characteristic of the restored Israel spoken of in Ezekiel 36:26–27: 'I will give you a new heart and put a new spirit in you; I will remove from you your heart of stone and give you a heart of flesh. And I will put my Spirit in you and move you to follow my decrees . . .'. The great features about a heart of flesh is that it can be penetrated by God. As Charles Bridges puts it, 'A needle pierces deeper into flesh than a sword into stone.' It is not difficult to correct someone who is sensitive to God. If such a person is in the wrong, he or she will accept his or her mistake and seek to do what is necessary to right that wrong.

In our work with Youth for Christ we have

many young full-time and volunteer staff. Some of them, filled with a lot of zeal and sometimes insufficient wisdom, make mistakes that may even have some bad affects on our work and reputation. This is something we have come to accept as a necessary difficulty one encounters when working with young people. Despite the damage to the work, we do not view these mistakes as being very serious. But sometimes when the person's error is pointed out, we find that he or she is not willing to accept responsibility for the problem. That to us *is* very serious, for it may indicate the lack of a teachable spirit. Charles Bridges, commenting on Proverbs 17:10, says, 'Reproof distinguishes the wise man from the fool.'

Because of the points given above, when we select staff for our work, one of the key qualities we look for is the quality of teachability or softheartedness. Teachability is a quality that cannot be gauged from an interview or a written application. Generally it is those who have worked closely with the person who know this. If a person has not been part of a group to which he or she is accountable, we would be very wary of taking that person on staff, however talented he or she may be. This is because the fact that this person has not been part of a group may indicate that he or she is not teachable.

The usual way to reject a rebuke is to give another explanation for the alleged error. It is not uncommon to find Christians giving explanations and excuses for actions that are not quite true. Most often, Christian leaders, not wanting the unpleasantness and pain of a confrontation, accept the explanation though they don't fully believe that what was said was the truth. That is very irresponsible on the part of the leader.

A false excuse or explanation for a sin is more serious than the sin itself. Nowhere in the Bible is it said that we are immune to sin. The Bible says over and over again that there is hope of healing for those who confess their sin. But those who don't accept that they have sinned have no hope. These principles are most clearly taught in 1 John 1:5 – 2:2. This familiar passage says there is hope for healing and fellowship with fellow Christians for those who walk in the light. The context shows that a key aspect of walking in the light is the willingness to accept that one has sinned and to confess that sin.

What we have said then is that the people who can benefit from a rebuke are those who, having a soft heart, are willing to accept their responsibility for an error. They will learn from their mistakes. They will receive God's forgiveness so that no blockage will prevent the grace of God from coming into their lives. Their futures are bright with the possibilities of God's rich grace.

How then can hard hearts become soft? How can those who have got accustomed to lying overcome the temptation to give an incorrect excuse or explanation for an error they have made? Is not lying one of the habits that is hardest to overcome? Looking at the lack of integrity that we see in the church today we may be filled with despair. But the passage we cited from Ezekiel gives us hope. We may not be able to develop soft hearts, but God can give us such hearts. Ezekiel 36:26 says, '*I will* give you a new heart, and put a new spirit within you; *I will* remove from you your heart of stone and give you a heart of flesh.' This is God speaking! What we cannot do, he can do in us.

The agent God often uses in creating in us a clean heart of integrity is the community of believers. As 1 John 1:7 points out, those who walk in the light have fellowship with one another. The converse of this is also true. Those who do not walk in the light cannot have fellowship with one another. If the community of believers is a truly biblical community, then someone who is not willing to face up to his or her sin will soon feel out of place. He or she must change and start walking in the light or leave the community. Praise God, the history of the church has many examples of people who stayed on and changed. The lack of integrity is a major problem in the church today. It is difficult to know who is truthful and who is not. If biblical community life is practised, you will find out. Those without integrity will either change or leave.

How alien teachability is in our society, where so much effort is made to put up a big show! The truly great people are always aware of how little they know. They will learn from anyone and will admit that they did so. They will accept their faults and be grateful when they are rebuked. This is because their aim in life is not to show how smart they are in relation to this world. They are followers of a servant Lord. Their aim is to serve. They would therefore be grateful when a hindrance to effective service is pointed out.

Evangelist D. L. Moody was fond of gardening and very proud of his flower beds in his home in Chicago. One day when he came home he found that his sons had romped on his flower beds and destroyed their beauty. He was infuriated and reprimanded his children very severely. After the reprimanding they went upstairs to their rooms. Some time later they heard their father coming up. The stairs were wooden and Moody was very heavy, so there was no doubt in the children's minds what the sound was. 'Now what?', they thought to themselves.

What their father said not only allayed their fears but also made a marked impression on them. He did not condone their error, but he confessed his own error in over-reacting and losing his temper and asked their forgiveness. Here was the most prominent evangelist and possibly the most famous Christian in the church in the West in his day. But he did not shrink from admitting he was wrong and asking the forgiveness of his children. That is a mark of one whose great desire in life is to fear God. No wonder God used him in such a powerful way so that, even now, almost ninety years after his death, the church is still enjoying the fruits of his labours.

It is clear that when we describe teachability we are not talking about the type of mentality of so-called 'professional students', that is, those who spend all their time studying just for the sake of it. The teachable learn so that they can put into practice what they learn. The end of our knowledge is obedience and service. And the end of obedience and service is the glory of God, not teachability. Our primary ambition is not to be teachable; it is to be Christlike and to bring glory to God!

Some supposedly teachable people don't launch out on any project for God, as they say they are not qualified to do it. Again, this is not the kind of teachability we are talking about. The refusal to launch out on fresh exploits for God often comes from pride. Such people won't try something new because they are reluctant to make mistakes and so make a fool of themselves. Sometimes this reluctance comes from laziness, they simply don't want to stretch themselves to launch out on new and difficult ventures.

Biblical teachability comes out of a burning desire to see God glorified in our lives and by our actions. Our passion for God's glory gives us the strength to face the humiliation of our faults. Our aim is not to show our abilities to the world, it is to show God's abilities. We should be glad to accept any help that we can get, in order to achieve that end, even though it may be a temporarily humbling experience for us.

# CHAPTER EIGHT

# FRIENDSHIP AND UNCONTROLLED TONGUES

We have, in this book, encountered some factors that can destroy friendships. Proverbs specifically mentions many instances where friendships can be destroyed by the uncontrolled use of the tongue. In this chapter we will look at some of these sins of the tongue.

## INSINCERE WORDS

The first text we will study describes insincere words. Proverb 27:14 says,

> If a man loudly blesses his neighbour early in
> the morning,
> it will be taken as a curse.

This verse has been understood in two ways. Since I find it difficult to decide between the two I will outline both.

## Inconsiderate blessing

The first interpretation is to take the act of blessing one's neighbour early in the morning as an example of inconsiderate behaviour. R. B. Y. Scott suggests that the reference to the blessing being given loudly may imply that the blessing roused the neighbour in the morning (presumably from his sleep). According to this interpretation the 'blessing' was imposed on the person in a way that became a hindrance, or as the proverb says 'a curse', to the one being blessed. In our eagerness to do what we believe is right we must not forget that the right thing must be done in a loving and sensitive way.

Let me list some examples of 'inconsiderate blessing'.

A young man is about to give his first major sermon before an august assembly. He has worked hard on the sermon and almost memorized it. Just before the service starts, a friend who knows the topic on which he is to speak, comes up and gives him a 'dose' of his 'great' insights on this topic. All that this eloquent speech does is to confuse the nervous, novice preacher. Even if the ideas were excellent, it is too late for him to include them in his carefully prepared sermon.

A young woman is going to a foreign country for further study. A friend wants to give her a parting gift. He knows that she is in need of money. He also knows that her bag must not weigh over 20 kilograms. But he decides not to give her money because that is not a gift that would be remembered. So he buys a framed painting and asks her to take it abroad with her so that she will remember their friendship. That is a selfish gift, for it added significantly to the weight of the bag.

An elderly person gets a heart attack in the middle of a church service. As he is being rushed to hospital, a Christian minister stops the helpers and says he wants to pray for the unconscious person. He delays them even though he could have said the same prayer without stopping the people on their way to the hospital.

An all-night prayer meeting is being held in the home of a sick woman. A main item of prayer is for her healing. But the people pray so loudly that they keep the woman awake, preventing her from getting much needed sleep.

These are examples of blessings that became curses, as our proverb says, because they have been given insensitively. This can happen because often our service becomes an expression of our selfishness. We get satisfaction from the service, so we do it whether the person needs it or not and whether the time and place are appropriate or not.

Let me give an example of a 'blessing' that was withheld by a person out of sensitivity to those who were to receive it, but in doing so gave them greater blessing. One Sunday two theological students went to minister in a church which was quite a distance from their theological school. Both were good preachers and were later to become prominent Christian leaders.

The plan for the Sunday was that in the morning service, one student would give a five-minute testimony and the other preach a full length sermon, reversing this process in the evening service. The morning service went ahead as planned. But at the evening service the preacher of the morning who was giving his testimony got carried away and testified for about the time of a full length sermon. It was a very powerful testimony.

The preacher of the evening got up to preach after the completion of a special musical item that followed the testimony. He sensed that the powerful testimony and song had made a marked impression upon the people and, therefore, that it would be more appropriate to give an invitation to discipleship than to preach his prepared sermon. He did this in about five minutes and many people came to the altar to commit their lives to Christ. He could not 'bless' the people with his preaching skills, but God blessed them with a much richer blessing!

Those who are inconsiderate in the way they try to help people will find it difficult to establish and keep close friendships. There is a selfish streak that enters into their relationships with others, making it difficult for them to open themselves to the self-giving which is a basic ingredient in a friendship relationship. In fact, because these 'inconsiderate helpers' impose themselves on others, people will avoid them, so that they can save themselves from the discomfort of having to endure the unwanted help.

## Insincere expressions of concern

The second way to interpret this proverb is to see it as an insincere expression of concern. Charles Bridges presents this view well: 'When a man exceeds all bounds of truth and decency, affecting pompous words and hyperbolical expressions, we cannot but suspect some sinister end.'

The underlying idea in this interpretation is that we should be suspicious of an exaggerated show of friendship. There may be a sinister motive behind it. The person may be trying to win us over for his or her own benefit. This is what lies behind the marketing practice used by business enterprises of giving gifts to prospective clients.

Sometimes the big show of friendship may be only a cover to hide the very shallow relationship that really exists. As Bridges says, 'Real friendship needs no such assurance.'

My mother once told us about an interesting thing that happened when she went to a function in Sri Lanka. It was many decades ago, in the days when couples would never express their affection to each other in public. There she saw a married couple give a public show of affection. A few weeks later this couple had separated and they were soon divorced. The unusual show of affection was probably an attempt to hide a troubled and shallow relationship.

How do these insincere expressions of concern become a curse, as the verse claims? A sad feature about most of us is that we often believe it when nice things are said about us and generally attribute pure motives to them. 'At least they understand me', we think to ourselves. This way we may believe in a falsehood and act upon it. We trust a person because we confuse the good feeling his or her words create in our minds with trustworthiness. We act on that trust and only later find out that we have been deceived and trapped into becoming part of an unscrupulous scheme. None of us are immune from a sense of vanity. We become very vulnerable when people pander to it.

Unscrupulous people can, by using their cunning methods, win partners for their devious schemes. But they cannot win true friends. Honesty is one of the basic requirements for a real friendship and they don't have it.

# GOSSIP

Gossip is one of the most serious sins of the tongue and its effects on friendship are mentioned often in Proverbs.

## Friendships broken

One of the most serious effects of gossip is the breaking of friendships. By gossiping a person can lose his or her own friends and also destroy the friendships of other people. Proverbs talks of both of these ways of separating friends.

Proverbs 17:9 says,

> He who covers over an offence promotes love,
> but whoever repeats the matter separates
> close friends.

(We will come back to this verse in the next chapter under the heading 'covering offences'.) We can talk to others about mistakes which a friend has made which we know about only because we are close to him or her. When our friend gets to know this he or she will take this as a case of betrayal. This is a sure way to lose the friendship. We have shown by our actions that we do not really care for him or her. We were willing to see our friend humiliated because of our perverse desire for the thrill that comes from gossiping. By our actions we have disqualified ourselves from friendship.

Proverbs 16:28 seems to suggest that the friendship broken is between people other than the gossip-monger.

A perverse man stirs up dissension,
and a gossip separates close friends.

Let me describe how this happens. Bill and Michael are good friends. Peter, the gossip-monger, tells Bill that Michael has said something nasty about Bill. Bill is so affected by this news that he feels he cannot trust Michael any more. Their friendship is broken because of what Peter told Bill.

This type of gossiping is one of the most common causes of illwill in the body of Christ today. Gossiping, and the resultant illwill, usually happen in three different ways. Perhaps it takes place most often *when a person talks too much*. There is usually no malicious intention behind this gossiping. The person has not learned to control his or her tongue. He or she has heard something, and may not even be sure of the facts, but talks about it without thinking much about the accuracy and the appropriateness of what is said. Such a person is a 'speech addict' who cannot control the habit of talking.

While there may be no malicious intent behind this, it is a sign of a spiritual malady. Jesus said, 'Out of the overflow of his heart his mouth speaks' (Luke 6:45). What comes out of our mouths is an indication of the health of our inner being. When gossip comes out it means that there is a need for more of the beauty of Jesus to become part of us.

Let me suggest a three-fold path to overcome this problem. First, because gossiping is a sign of inner ugliness, we need to be feeding our minds on the thoughts that will fill us with the beauty of Christ. Paul's advice in Philippians 4:8 is a very appropriate antidote for this malady:

117

> Whatever is true, whatever is noble, whatever is right, whatever is pure, whatever is lovely, whatever is admirable – if anything is excellent or praiseworthy – think about such things.

Inner beauty is not formed in us overnight. We must linger with God's Word so that his thoughts can fill our beings. We must be sure that our minds do not have the cancer of hate and the spirit of unforgiveness which destroy beauty. Such attitudes must be surrendered to God and his help enlisted in our pursuit of Christlikeness.

Secondly, we need to be very conscious of the problem and be on our guard lest our tongue slips into the old habit. However much time we spend with God, we live in a fallen world and illwill is part of the environment. It is so easy to win a hearing with gossip. Even when Christian leaders meet, this is a topic that is generally sure to interest everyone present. So let's turn our attention to one of those key verses in Scripture, which if followed, will bring much beauty to the life of the church. How appropriate for us is the advice of Psalm 141:3: 'Set a guard over my mouth, O Lord, keep watch over the door of my lips.'

Thirdly, when we realize that we have spoken out of turn we should go to God, ask his forgiveness and do all we can to right the wrong. We may need to write a letter asking the person who heard us to forgive us for polluting his or her mind and appealing to him or her to try and erase it from memory. Or we may visit the person we spoke to with the same intention. This step suggests that we are serious about the problem, and it is a sure

118

remedy. God will honour such seriousness of purpose. The inconvenience of going through this long process of restitution will serve as a deterrent to indulge further in gossip.

What I have said above is very basic. And yet the problem of gossip continues to cause much havoc among Christians. Often those guilty of gossip are respected leaders. It is clear that Christians are not grappling adequately with this issue. Therefore, it would be good to upgrade, or should we say downgrade, gossip to the status of being a major problem in the church.

The second way gossip destroys friendships is also a non-malicious way. It comes out of *immature loyalty*. Here's an example of this type of gossip. A young Christian who is very loyal to the leader hears that a friend of the leader has said something bad about him or her. Through loyalty to the leader the person rushes to him or her and relates the incident, 'This is what your friend said about you.' This places the leader in a very difficult position. He or she cannot erase the report from his or her mind. Ideally, he or she should check with the friend whether this is true. But sometimes he or she may be hindered from doing this because a problem has come between these two people already. Usually this is what happens when loyal people tell such stories to their leaders. The rift is widened. And the process of healing is made so much harder.

The Christians who do this must be told that this behaviour is wrong; that they should go and talk to the person who made the statement against the leader before going to the leader. That would save so much unnecessary heartache. It is another

119

instance where control has to be exercised over the tongue.

The third way gossip takes place is different to the two we have discussed so far. These two were devoid of a serious intention to hurt anyone. The third, however, is done *out of malice*.

A good way to describe those who gossip maliciously is to contrast them with those who do not. The latter are people who are overwhelmed by gratitude to God. Because of their gratitude a sweetness of disposition becomes part of their nature. They are so grateful for the way that God has been good to them that now they gladly give their energy towards bringing some of the love they have experienced to others. These are the people whose fulfilment in life comes from God. The love of God has removed bitterness and replaced it with gratitude for healing grace. They may be people who have had a lot of problems, but have found the grace of God sufficient to face the pain of these problems. Such people are not angry with the world, and so have no desire to harm people.

But there are many even in the church, who have not let the grace of God heal them of their hurts. They approach life with anger – anger about the way they have been treated. This anger finds an outlet in gossip. They get a certain fulfilment from saying bad things about other people. The anger they have towards those who have hurt them is unleashed in unkind words said about others.

I'm sure you have heard children express their satisfaction over some misfortune that someone had, at a time when they are angry and frustrated. One of my (now famous) angry statements as a child was, 'It was very good that Mr Menzies fell off the chair.' Mr Menzies was my aunt's piano teacher. One day, during a piano lesson, the chair he was sitting on broke and he fell down, much to the embarrassment of my grandparents at whose house this happened. I had nothing at all against Mr Menzies, but it was an unfortunate incident, and in my angry condition I found that to express my satisfaction over this incident was a good way to vent my frustration. Adults don't usually say such silly things. But they do something very similar – they gossip. They vent their anger about the way people have treated them by saying bad thing about others.

Malicious gossipers have an even more serious spiritual problem than those who gossip because they haven't learned to control their tongues. When Christians see a fellow Christian do this, they need to approach the person and talk about it with a view to being an agent of healing in his or her life.

## Betraying confidence

There is a type of gossip which is singled out and specifically mentioned in Proverbs. That is the practice of sharing with others things that have been shared by a friend in confidence.

A gossip betrays a confidence,
　but a trustworthy man keeps a secret.
(Proverbs 11:13)

A gossip betrays a confidence;
　so avoid a man who talks too much.
(Proverbs 20:19)

A person who keeps a secret is an honourable person. Honourable people will not share with others things that were told them in confidence, even if they have to pay a price.

> If you argue your case with a neighbour,
>> do not betray another man's confidence,
> or he who hears it may shame you
>> and you will never lose your bad
>>> reputation.
>
> (Proverbs 25:9–10)

When we are in a tight spot in a court case we may be able to clear ourselves by sharing something that was told to us in confidence. Proverbs says we must not use this method even if we suffer from our refusal to do it.

Christian leaders will often encounter this type of problem. If they are proper leaders they will know many things about those in their group which cannot be shared in public. Often in a conversation, there may come a point where sharing these things would really help to enlighten those who are there. But we must strenuously resist the temptation to do this.

Perhaps the worst way to break a confidence is to talk about a secret in a sermon. However appropriate an incident may be in illustrating the point we are making, we must not use it if it will break a confidence. We may sometimes use the story by modifying it so that the person's identity is not revealed. For example, I may speak of an experience which I had, as if it happened to someone else. I may start something like this: 'A young man came to a Christian minister with this problem . . .'. The audience does not know *I* am that minister. Some of the details of the story could be altered so that it becomes a parable based on fact. If the story can't be modified in this way, then it should not be used.

Dr David Seamands dealt with this problem in his book, *Healing for Damaged Emotions*. In it he uses a lot of illustrations from his counselling ministry. But first he got permission from those about whom he was going to write. Then he changed their names and held back some of the other details that might result in the reader identifying the person who was being written about.

## Avoid gossips

In Proverbs 20:19 we are asked to avoid those who betray a confidence. Gossips not only separate friends, they also separate themselves from their own friends. This insatiable desire to talk causes them to break confidences. So people do not trust them and they stop regarding themselves as their friends. True friendships include the sharing of some confidential matters, but these people have been shown to be unable to handle the responsibility of keeping secrets. Thus they forfeit the right to be a listener of confidential matters.

What an irony this is! People who talk too much end up not having anyone to involve in the type of conversation that really matters to them – the affirming conversations that friends have with each other. This is what banishes our loneliness and brings to us the great blessings that friendship gives. The irony is that gossips indulge in gossip in order to have someone listen to them. They may get listeners, but they won't get what they need –

friends. They may get a malicious satisfaction from winning a hearing through their unsavoury talk, but, because they acted against God's way for a fulfilled life, their misery and loneliness are compounded.

Proverbs 18:8 advises us to avoid gossipers because of the strong influence gossip can have us:

> The words of a gossip are like choice morsels;
> they go down to a man's inmost parts.

This same proverb appears again in Proverbs 26:22 also. The words of a gossip are described as being 'choice' or 'delicious' morsels. Most people like to hear a 'juicy' story about someone. As Robert Alden comments, 'The point is, gossip seems so "delicious" to us that we are powerless to resist it.' In fact, one who gossips is generally sure to win a hearing.

Our eagerness to hear destructive rumours is a sign of our fallenness. It gives us a certain satisfaction to know that others are also sinners. It temporarily soothes our insecurity. But this is sinful and unloving. As Paul says, 'Love does not delight in evil' (1 Corinthians 13:6). Of course, the security it gives us is fleeting. True security comes from knowing that we have been forgiven in Christ, considered righteous and accepted as full members of the family of God.

Proverbs 18:8 and 26:22 not only say that the words of a gossip taste delicious, they also say that these words 'go down to a man's inward parts'. Kenneth Aitken explains this statement clearly:

> Once digested the whisperer's words are
> never quite forgotten. They remain

124

indelibly imprinted on the mind. So while the hearer might keep it to himself, the very fact that he heard means the damage has been done; for thereafter his attitude to and relationship with the whisperer's victim will never quite be the same.

Because of these lasting effects of gossip, good people learn to leave the scene when a gossip talks. In fact, we are told that to listen deliberately to such tales is a wicked thing to do:

A wicked man listens to evil lips;
a liar pays attention to a malicious tongue.

(Proverbs 17:4)

These strong words from Proverbs end this section, reminding the reader that an uncontrolled tongue disqualifies a person from friendship and greatly dishonours God. Let us regard it as a destructive force and make a concerted effort to fight it.

## SINS OF THE TONGUE SHOULD BE CONFRONTED

The Scriptures give a very important place to the havoc caused by the unsanctified use of the tongue. Two of the books that focus on practical hints for daily life, Proverbs and James, have a lot to say about this. Therefore, Christians need to be confronting this issue seriously. This should be one of the areas where we rebuke fellow Christians.

Yet often we feel we don't have the freedom to confront a fellow Christian on something like this. Generally, uncontrolled tongues are allowed to go unchecked and so cause much destruction. If we don't have the freedom to confront gossipers with the seriousness of what they are doing, that is an indication that the fellowship has moved far away from the biblical model. If a church or some other fellowship within the body of Christ realizes that it has come to this point, then it's time to get really serious with God. I have used the word 'serious' many times in this chapter. This is because the church is, among other things, a community of people who are seriously intent on pleasing God.

Alas, many churches seem to be so influenced by the entertainment orientated society of today that this seriousness seems to have been eclipsed by the desire to 'somehow keep Christians satisfied by giving them an enjoyable time'. The leaders are afraid that if they point out these errors some members will leave and go 'to the church down the road'. That would be considered a big failure to the church. Besides, churches often have not been so serious about fellowship as to develop an atmosphere that is conducive to confronting people about their personal behaviour. The people come to church to get blessed, and then leave. Some members will volunteer their services for some of the programmes of the church. The leaders are grateful that they do that. They would not want to lose their help. But if they are confronted about an issue in their life they might get upset and leave. So it is deemed advisable not to talk about such things.

My point is that the church should be seriously addressing the sins that surface in its body life. And sins of the tongue surface often. Gossips must be made to feel uncomfortable with gossiping and at the same time be showered with the holy care of reproof, counsel and instruction that will help them 'kick the habit'. Sincere Christians won't leave a church that demonstrates true concern for them. In fact, such a church would not need to use entertainment to keep the crowd. If people know that the church is truly committed to them, they will reciprocate by being committed to the church. They will stay, not because they are entertained, but because they have a sense of ownership. They are committed. Commitment can stand the test of painful experiences. In fact, when there is commitment, painful experiences serve to make the tie even deeper.

Again we come to the principle that costly commitment is not as unpragmatic as it seems. The results may take longer to come and the experiences are sometimes stretching, but what emerges is far more satisfying and lasting. The other methods that have replaced commitment are no match for the real thing! They will leave the church impoverished and ineffective.

# CHAPTER NINE

# THE COMFORT OF A FRIEND

The last two chapters were somewhat severe in that they dealt with the wounding that is a part of friendship and the destruction of friendship through the wrong use of the tongue. My original plan had been to end the book with the chapter on how friendships are destroyed. Then I realized that because friendship is such a beautiful thing it would be inappropriate to end the book on such a sour note. So I kept the chapter on the comfort of friendship to the last, so the reader could finish the book with a sense of the glory of friendship.

## COVERING OFFENCES

In an earlier chapter we said that we have the responsibility to point out the faults of our friends, but we are also called to cover their offences.

He who covers an offence promotes love,
>    but whoever repeats the matter separates
>    close friends.

>                                   (Proverbs 17:9)

Similarly,

> Love covers over all wrongs.
>                                   (Proverbs 10:12)

What does it mean to cover offences? Other passages in Proverbs help us to eliminate the idea that it means hushing up a person's sins or being reluctant to rebuke a person when he or she does wrong. The Scriptures also tell us that we must publicly rebuke the sins of those, especially leaders, whose sins have a public effect in bringing dishonour to God (1 Timothy 5:20).

The antithesis of covering sin, as presented in Proverbs 17:9, helps us understand what is meant by these words. After mentioning the need to cover offences, the proverb says: 'Whoever repeats the matter separates close friends.' The two parallel statements in a Hebrew proverb are usually closely allied, which is the case here. Repeating a matter is the opposite of covering a sin. To repeat a matter may mean either harping on it, which is how the NEB translates it, or tale-telling, as most of the other translations put it.

In both cases the root of the matter is the biblical understanding of forgiveness. Once a person has confessed a sin and received forgiveness, God does not remember the sin any more (Jeremiah 31:34). Similarly, we as the followers of God's ways must forget sins that have been forgiven.

Before we can forget a sin, it must first be

forgiven. That means the sin must be acknowledged by the wrongdoer and responsibility accepted for it. Otherwise there will be no forgiveness. And there can be no real fellowship either. 1 John 1:7 says, 'If we walk in the light, as he is in the light, we have fellowship with one another.' If a person refuses to walk in the light, which is what the refusal to confess our sins is, then there can be no fellowship. But to those who will walk in the light, the message of 1 John 1:7 is, 'The blood of Jesus, his Son, purifies us from all sin.'

When a person is cleansed by the blood of Jesus, his or her sin has been forgotten. Then we who are servants of God must forget the sin too. This does not mean we are to be unaware of a person's weaknesses. But it does mean that we treat the person as if the sin were truly in the past. We don't bring it up in a way that is damaging to the person.

I was once in a confrontation with a colleague. It was a necessary, though unpleasant, confrontation. I was not getting through to the colleague and in an effort to press home my case, I referred to an issue that had been settled many years before. That served to complicate the issue greatly and made the resolution of the problem much more painful. It was an unnecessary point brought in to gain a quick, but cheap, advantage. I praise the Lord that, because his grace was bigger than the problem, the resolution was complete and the ensuing unity as deep as ever. But I learned an important lesson. We must not harp on sins that have been cleansed by the blood of Christ.

If harping on cleansed sins is a bad practice, talking about them to others is worse. This is a betrayal of friendship. People often share confidential things with us about errors they have made and sins they have committed. As people love to hear gossip and we love to have people to listen to us speak, we may be tempted to share what was told us in confidence. Often this slips out of our mouth without much pre-planning.

What then does it mean to cover sin? We have seen that it means we must not talk about it without a biblically endorsed reason for doing so. But there is more to it than this. Charles Martin suggests that covering sin means 'keeping matters discreetly until reconciliation is achieved'. How often we bring a private disagreement or opinion about the actions of a person out into the public without first confronting the person directly. When we act hastily in this way the chances of us being an influence for good in the situation are greatly reduced. We have lost our credibility by our hasty action.

So the action of covering sin has to do primarily with the control of our tongue. This is an area that we must constantly battle, however mature we may think we are. Our constant prayer should be, 'Set a guard over my mouth, O LORD; keep watch over the door of my lips' (Psalm 141:3).

## WHEN WE FALL

Our next principle comes from a familiar passage on friendship in Ecclesiastes:

> If one falls down,
>     his friend can help him up.
> But pity the man who falls
>     and has no-one to help him up.
>
> (Ecclesiastes 4:10)

Michael Eaton points out that the background to this statement is a fall into a ditch or pit: 'A lonely fall might be fatal, especially at night.' Eaton goes on to say that the proverb 'looks beyond physical mishap' to 'slips of judgment and other types of "falling by the wayside"'.

## Discouragement after failure

Failure makes us vulnerable to all sorts of attacks which are sometimes worse than the failure itself. At such a time friends are a great help in putting things in perspective. Failure can make us over-discouraged. Because a person preached badly on one occasion he may conclude that preaching is something he is not called to do. Friends who are not so emotionally devastated by the incident will help knock some sense into him and show him that the situation is not at bad as he thinks.

Friends may help us get sufficient courage to try again at an exam we failed on our first attempt, or to keep singing even though the first time we gave a solo turned out to be a disaster. I remember reading that the first public solo given by the great gospel singer George Beverly Shea was a disaster. But he did not give up singing because of that. He went on to become one of the English-speaking world's best loved gospel singers.

An even more extreme form of over-discouragement is when we think that because we have failed in one area, we are failures in all of life. For example, if we lose our job, we might conclude that we are completely worthless. At such times too our friends help us realize that there is more to life than one's job or whatever area we failed in. This gives us the courage to start 'picking up the pieces' of life so that we can get off to a fresh start.

Hudson Taylor was one of the great missionary heroes of the last century. Yet after being in China for a little less than two years he was in a state of deep discouragement. His missionary society had failed to keep its promise to support him. The established missionaries in China were critical of his unorthodox methods. His girl friend in England had written that she feared that she did not love him. The British consul had ordered him to stop work in one of the towns where he was working. He wrote to his mother, 'My heart is sad, sad. I do not know what to do.'

At this stage a godly Scottish missionary named William Burns, who was about twenty years Hudson Taylor's senior, befriended him. They travelled, preached, and prayed together for seven months. Burns was God's answer for Taylor's discouragement. John Pollock, in his biography of Taylor, writes: 'Burns saved Taylor from himself. Rejected by conventional missionaries he might have grown into an isolated prig, an individualist adventuring in steadily contracting circles, leaving behind nothing but a few converts and an awkward memory . . . . [He] received from Burns an imprint which was never effaced' (page 61).

Taylor went on to found the China Inland Mission whose ministry over the years is one of the most exciting stories in missionary history. Eighty-three years after Taylor's death it still operates, though under a new name, Overseas Missionary Fellowship. Its old urgency to share Christ with the lost and its commitment to stick uncompromisingly to biblical principles continue to be the distinguishing marks of the movement.

Many Christians who launched out on difficult projects have either given up or compromised their principles when they faced the inevitable discouragement that such ventures entail. We hear of missionaries who tried to reach an unreached group but returned after a few years, totally discouraged by their lack of visible fruit and not willing to go back. Most of us know of Christians who went to work in areas usually avoided by Christians, like politics and trade. And after a time, their Christian stand was compromised.

We also know, however, of those who did stick uncompromisingly to their original commitments. Most of these people had other Christians to whom they were accountable and who would encourage them along the path of obedience. The classic example of this is William Wilberforce. As a member of the British parliament he led a long campaign to abolish the slave trade in Britain. He experienced the joy of success only after many years. He suffered from frequent migraine attacks possibly brought on by the strain of a bruising battle. But right through this battle he had a closely-knit group of Christians, mostly members of his church in Clapham, who encouraged him, prayed for him and mustered prayer support all over England. The fascinating life of this group, the Clapham Sect, has been the subject of a number of books.

There is a great need today for Christians to go into 'difficult professions', like reaching the unreached, secular journalism, law, politics, high school teaching, trade, social welfare, finance and business. But those going into such professions are going to face many obstacles and discouragements.

It would be dangerous to go into such work without the support of some Christian friends. That is why I do not recommend sending out workers to start a Christian work in a completely new area alone.

## In times of moral failure

Friends are extremely valuable at times of moral failure also. Many Christians are struggling with moral problems they don't know how to handle. They feel reluctant to tell just anyone about it. They are often caught in a trap of failure that keeps getting worse as time goes by. This is a particular problem with leaders, for they may not be able to share their problems freely.

The problem may be lust, or problems that are developing in the relationship with the person's spouse. It may be that his or her devotions have gone dry, or that business with his or her job or ministry means there is little time left for the family. If these problems are not dealt with adequately they can trap the Christian into a descending spiral of defeat and discouragement. Soon he or she loses confidence in his or her ability to handle the problem. Others see this person work hard, and they think things are going fine in his or her life. Suddenly there is a big crash, such as a moral scandal or a divorce and people are shocked and saddened.

When we are struggling with a moral problem and share it with someone we trust the usual immediate response is one of great relief. That relief itself may clear a lot of the air and take away the heavy load that we were living under. That helps us to look at the problem in a more constructive way.

We may find out that lust is something that leaders are not immune to and be led to ways that would help us overcome it. The accountability that we have affirmed with our friend may be precisely what we needed to help us stop watching unedifying television programmes or videos, that are so accessible. The fact that we have to report to our friend about our TV-watching 'performance' will help us resist the temptation to watch what we should not watch.

A simple word of advice a friend gives a struggling Christian may be all that is needed to help him or her snap back victoriously from the problem. For example, a young woman finds that she is getting attracted to a married man who helps her in some way. She shares it with a friend whose advice gives her the courage to take the difficult step of refusing the help. Once that step is taken she quickly returns to her original state of spiritual vitality.

What we have said above underscores the importance of Paul's admonition in Galatians 6:1-2: 'Brothers, if someone is caught in a sin, you who are spiritual should restore him gently ... Carry each other's burdens, and in this way you will fulfil the law of Christ.'

## ACCOUNTABILITY VERSUS SUPERFICIAL FELLOWSHIP

We must note that the context of Ecclesiastes 4:10 (that is, verses 9–12) is of people working close to each other. Verse 9 speaks of those who have a good return for their work – that is workmates. Verse 11 speaks of two who lie together – that is a married couple or travelling mates who sleep close to each other in order to keep warm. Verse 12 speaks of two people who face an enemy together.

There is a very significant implication that we can draw from the above evidence. Those we live and work close to are the best people to provide us with the blessings of companionship. If we are married, our spouse would be the most important in this regard. Another level of sharing would be with our colleagues in ministry. They would form what has come to be known as our accountability group.

However, there seems to be a trend among Christians towards forming our accountability group from people who are outside our group of close associates. We have a business relationship with our associates and a sharing relationship with those in the accountability group. This again is a carry over to the life of the church from a secular model of management.

Another trend we see is that, lacking the deep blessing of spiritual accountability, we seem to be choosing shallow fellowship instead. Week-end retreats have become very popular in many countries. People share about their lives quite openly with strangers who happen to be put into the same group at the retreat. There is value in this. And yet we must not confuse it with spiritual accountability. It is too shallow a fellowship to be called accountability.

It is not always easy to be frank with those with whom we work closely. It may slow down the work because time has to be spent breaking down the barriers that inevitably arise when people work close to each other and which prevent us being of one mind. If we did not have such high expectations from the fellowship then we could ignore the differences and go ahead with our work. In this way we would do a bigger volume of work for the kingdom and thus be a more 'successful' organization, but that success has been measured from a worldly standard. Success in the kingdom is determined by whether the work has been done in God's way. The testimony of Scripture is surely that being 'of one mind' is a necessary ingredient for a ministry team. This was demonstrated in our earlier discussion on team ministry (see chapter two, especially the section on 'Friendship at team meetings').

Our conclusion is that ministry teams that meet God's standards place a high emphasis upon 'being of one mind'. But clearing barriers to fellowship may take a lot of time and thus threaten the technical proficiency of the group. For example, practice time or sleep could get eaten into, leaving the team somewhat unprepared or tired during the programme. But by paying that price, we will have gained a spiritual power that is more capable of reaping eternal fruit than technical excellence.

Being spiritually accountable to our colleagues also brings with it a lot of responsibility. When our accountability group is outside our immediate circle of colleagues, we can share our problems with the group, but we will not generally be challenged. If, for example, we are doing something wrong which has caused a problem, we will invariably give the group our version of the problem which may not be very accurate. Based on that misinformation, our group may back us when they should be rebuking us!

If the problem is shared with people who work close to us, there is a greater chance of the group challenging us and helping us along the path to perfection. They will see if we really are making an effort to solve the problem. So the responsibility associated with sharing with people who are close to us is greater than that with people who are not so close to us. It may be uncomfortable and humiliating at times, but that is the price of spiritual accountability.

Usually the accountability that we have within 'responsible' Christian organizations is confined to the handling of finances and the performance of one's duties in terms of his or her job description. We are making a plea to add to this the all important aspect of spiritual accountability.

As in many spheres of activity, integrating the different facts of life is not easy. So we prefer to separate them. Hence we have one group for spiritual accountability and anther group for vocational accountability. Bringing them together 'under one roof' may result in a lot of friction. But from that friction will come a power, and an ability to penetrate those whose problems run very deep. Much of our shallow performances, despite all their technical competence, are failing to penetrate truly the people and the culture with the gospel of Christ.

## WARMTH IN TIMES OF NEED

Friends not only help us when we fall, they also bring the warmth of affirming concern when the cold realities of life in a hostile world hit us. The philosopher who wrote Ecclesiastes goes on to say,

If two lie down together, they will keep warm.
But how can one keep warm alone?.
(Ecclesiastes 4:11)

As we have said, this verse could refer to the husband-wife relationship. But more likely it refers to travellers who sleep together in the cold winter nights of Israel in order to keep warm (Eaton). Unfortunately the rise of homosexuality in some cultures has made this type of activity seem somewhat unnatural. But what we have here is a picture of companionship in times of adversity and grief. This is a world where we are often battered by hostile forces. The cold realities of misunderstanding, opposition, grief and failure often hit us with great intensity. What a comfort friends are at such times.

It is important to note again that the blessing of comfort described here is available to those who have a friend close enough to them to know what the problem is. I have heard people complain that there was no-one to help them when they were going through a crisis. They blame the church for not caring for them. Indeed the church should try to find out who is sick or in some difficulty from among its fold. But often the reason why the church does not know about their problem is because they have kept aloof from the people and the others have no way of finding out about their problems. They chose not to develop close friendships because they were too much of a nuisance. They preserved their privacy, but missed the blessings of companionship.

Those who choose a lifestyle that includes cultivating close friendships and ministering in an open hearted way with people, become vulnerable to much inconvenience and pain. But when they face hardship they usually find that there are people willing to bear their burdens and help out sacrificially. There may be exceptions to this rule, as in the case of Paul's final imprisonment (2 Timothy 4:9–11). But generally in times of difficulty those who open their hearts to others find the fulfilment of Christ's promise that 'no-one who has left home or brothers or sisters or mother or father or children or fields for me and the gospel will fail to receive a hundred times as much in this present age (homes, brothers, sisters, mothers, children and fields – and with them persecutions) and in the age to come, eternal life' (Mark 10:29–30). Though the sacrifice mentioned here by Christ is not exactly the same, the principle, that God provides sufficient grace to face up to hardship, applies always in the experience of God's faithful servants.

Note that Jesus says that God provides us with 'brothers, sisters, mothers [and] children'. These are ties of love and commitment which are a great source of strength and comfort in times of hardship. Jesus, of course, is very realistic when he adds 'and with them persecutions'. We are not immune to hardship, but the hardship provides God with an opportunity to shower upon us his sufficient grace. This becomes a great encouragement and incentive to a firmer commitment to the way of the cross. The grace, as we said, is often mediated through fellow-Christians. Thus we realize that the price for a life of sacrificial service to others is well worth paying.

The statement that God is no man's debtor is always true. We may seem to be deprived of some earthly comforts, like our privacy, because we chose the path of spiritual accountability to a group. But God always ensures we have that 'life . . . to the full' that Christ came to give us (John 10:10). We are fulfilled people. One of the means through which God mediates this fulfilment to us is our friends, for God made us as communal beings and therefore community is one of the basic ingredients of a fulfilled life.

Fulfilment is what people look for so much, but in the wrong places. In fact, many people avoid the commitment which true friendship requires, thinking that such commitment is a hindrance to fulfilment. That is the extent to which the false philosophy of 'self-fulfilment' has blinded us from seeing where true fulfilment is to be found.

## STRENGTH TO DEFEND OURSELVES

The next verse in the Ecclesiastes passage (chapter 4:12) describes how friends help us when we have to defend ourselves:

> Though one may be overpowered,
> two can defend themselves.

When we are active in doing God's will, we often face attacks from hostile forces. When we have other people together with us in these battles we are much stronger. The verse goes on to describe this strength vividly:

> A cord of three strands is not quickly broken.

Some of the forces we battle with are earthly, others are directly satanic. We will look briefly at both these areas of battle.

A simple illustration explains how friends help us in our battle against earthly forces. The missionary arm of our ministry has been doing pioneering evangelism in some completely Buddhist villages.

People from these villages have been converted and baptized, bringing great joy to us. But it has also opened us to attacks from those who are unhappy about people giving up the national religion to follow another. One day I got a letter from a government official challenging our actions and asking for the baptismal certificates of those who were baptized. He had a lot of authority in the villages in which we were working, so I was very concerned.

Before I took any action, I showed the letter to my colleagues and to some of our board members. One of them pointed out that this letter had not come on a government letterhead, a fact that I had not noticed. This meant it did not have the status of an official letter. Another said he knew a Christian constitutional lawyer who could give us advice on the matter. He took it to this lawyer who advised us that the wisest thing to do was not to respond to the letter. The matter ended with that. Now years after the incident we realize that this was indeed the wisest thing to do.

Often when we are attacked, we lash out in defence without thinking about the consequences of our action. These sudden reactions usually complicate matters and do not help in working towards a solution. Let's look at another common occurrence. Someone criticizes a Christian leader unfairly. The leader is so upset about this that he or she wants to respond to the criticism immediately, and writes a letter in his or her defence and circulates it widely. Most of those who receive the letter do not even know about the criticism. The letter was written in such a provocative way that it creates a stir in the community. The letter responding to criticism did much more to damage the credibility of the leader than the criticism itself. A true friend could have helped the leader to act more sensibly under fire, by convincing him or her that publicising the controversy would be of more damage than help.

Lone people often act irrationally when attacked. They lash out in their insecurity, perhaps in an effort to feel strong when really they feel weak. They need someone who will drive some sense into them and help them to avoid these irrational reactions.

The principle of the value of friends when we are under fire is applicable in many other areas of life, such as trouble in our places of work. Often when we are under fire at our work-place, our first reaction could be to look for another job. Friends can help us respond in a wiser way to this crisis.

While Satan may be behind the attacks that come to us from human sources, he sometimes attacks in a more direct manner. Paul describes this in Ephesians 6:12: 'Our struggle is not against flesh and blood, but against the rulers, against the authorities, against the powers of this dark world and against spiritual forces of evil in the heavenly realms.' Paul's advice is to 'put on the full armour of God, so that when the evil day comes, you may be able to stand your ground' (Ephesians 6:13). In the next four verses he goes on to describe what this armour is.

There is something we often overlook when we study this popular passage in Ephesians about spiritual warfare. The 'you' does not refer to a lone soldier carrying out a war valiantly against Satan. The 'you' is in the plural. Unfortunately in the English language 'you' can be either singular or plural, and we usually think of it as being in the singular. What Ephesians 6 describes is an army at war against Satan's forces. That's how God intends us to carry out our battles against demonic forces – as an army.

When we think of our battle against Satan we usually think of temptation to personal sin. This is indeed a very important aspect of our battle, but sometimes our battle may be a more direct and public confrontation with demonic forces. We face this, for example, when we minister in an area that had been under the control of demonic powers. Animistic villages in the 'Third World' and Satanic cults in the West are examples of these spheres of activity. We may be called upon to minister to a person who is demon possessed.

At such times of direct confrontation with Satan and his armies it is particularly important for us not to go alone. We become very vulnerable to the attacks of Satan because we are directly invading his territory. He will work extra hard to defeat us. In such battles we are prone to problems of fear, discouragement, and making hasty judgments. Friends can help us overcome such problems. It is a sad fact that many Christian workers who have battled directly with the demonic have fallen into sexual sin. This is but one example of Satan's strategy to attack those who dare to battle with him. In our chapter on 'Wisdom through friends' we showed that spiritual accountability is a very effective antidote to sexual failure.

The thrust of Ephesians 6:13 then is that we must not try to battle alone. If it is absolutely impossible to find someone to be with us when we are in a battle, God will surely provide sufficient grace. But we must always remember that this is not the norm.

The norm for battling in the Christian life is in the context of a fellowship or army of believers.

Sometimes, when we are forced by unavoidable circumstances to battle alone, we can get others to support us in prayer. James O. Fraser was forced, much against his wishes, to do a lot of lone pioneering work among the Lisus in the mountains of China. Yet Fraser had a band of friends in England, his home country, who were committed to pray for him. He faithfully kept them motivated to pray by sending these friends regular reports of the work and discourses on the type of prayer that was needed to help in the challenges he faced. *Mountain Rain*, a recent biography of James Fraser by Eileen Grossman, contains many helpful hints on how to get others to join us in our battles through wrestling in prayer for us, as Epaphras did for the Colossians (Colossians 4:12).

## FRIENDSHIP AND PERSONAL PROBLEMS

What we have been saying in this chapter is that when we have personal problems the best people to help are those who are close to us, like our friends and relatives. Today when people have personal problems they often go to a specialist like a psychiatrist. Thomas Szasz, who is himself a psychiatrist, has said that psychotherapy is the purchase of friendship. He does not mean, of course, that friends can solve all the problems that people take to psychotherapists. We need specialists for extreme problems. But many of the less extreme problems about which people consult psychiatrists and other specialists could be even more effectively handled by friends.

The Christian psychologist Gary Collins calls this 'peer counselling'. In his book, *How To Be A People Helper*, he shows that studies have revealed that the so-called lay helper is as effective and sometimes more effective than the professional counsellor. He gives five reasons that give friends an advantage over professionals in counselling (pages 58–59). He says that in contrast to professionals, the peer helper (a) is closer to the helpee, knows him or her as a friend, and is thus better able to understand the problem and to pick up non-verbal clues or demonstrate a sincere empathy; (b) is more often available and is thus able to provide help consistently and whenever it is especially needed; (c) often knows about the helpee's family, work situation, life-style, beliefs or neighbourhood and can therefore take a more active part in guiding decisions or helping to change his or her life situation; (d) is able to communicate in language – including slang or native tongue – which the helpee can easily understand; and (e) is more down-to-earth, relaxed, open, informal and inclined to introduce a tension-relieving humour.

Yet few people are willing to pay the price in terms of the time needed to help a friend with a personal problem. It takes time and patience to listen to friends sharing their problems, to comfort those who are sorrowful and to counsel those in need of guidance. Helping friends to overcome personality problems is a special challenge requiring a lot of commitment. Because many are not willing to give that type of commitment the only recourse some people have is to go to a specialist. They purchase friendship by paying professional fees.

Ron Lee Davis gives a good example of the power of the Christian community to act as a healing agent in his book, *Gold in the Making* (pages 77–79). There was a woman in North America, pseudonymed Ruth, who had been an active worker in her church, having served as Christian Education Director. But Ruth became severely depressed and had to quit her job and her work in her church. She withdrew herself from her friendships and social contacts and began to take large doses of tranquilizers prescribed by her physician. She then sought help from a psychiatrist and also from her pastor.

While she was in this desperate state her pastor had to leave to serve in another church at quite a distance. He decided that before he left he would do all he could to help Ruth. He visited her psychiatrist who told him, 'There is absolutely nothing we can do for Ruth. She's in a state of deep depression, and it is my opinion that she will remain in that depression for the rest of her life. No one will ever be able to help Ruth.'

However, the pastor did not give up on Ruth. He referred Ruth to one of the house groups within the congregation. Ron Davis describes this as 'a group of eight or ten people who had committed themselves to each other to study the Bible together, to pray for each other and support each other, to be open, honest and sensitive to each other, and to hold all sharing within the group in strict confidence.' This is a group that sought to model the type of friendship we have been describing in this book.

The people in this group were not told anything about Ruth's problems. They became her friends.

Three months after joining the group, she was off prescribed drugs completely. Within six months she had returned to work. Today she is cured of her depression. Friends helped her to become whole again.

## THE PLEASANTNESS OF FRIENDS

We have come to the end of the book! Many things have been said about friendship. You may have been surprised at how much Proverbs says on the topic and how relevant it is for today. There is still one more text to look at. It shows how friends bring joy to our life and compares it to the joy that perfume and incense brings to the heart. I want to end by quoting that verse and expressing my prayer and wish that you, the reader, would experience in your life the joy of having friends who are closer than a brother.

> Perfume and incense bring joy to the heart,
>     and the pleasantness of one's friend springs
>         from his earnest counsel.
>
> (Proverbs 27:9)

# ORGANIZATIONAL GOALS AND OUR PERSONAL VISION

In this book we have talked a lot about how people should be committed to each other and to the groups to which they belong. But does that stifle the personal growth of the individuals in the group? What should we do if a person in our group has a different vision than that which the group has? What about the person who has gifts that should be used outside the group too? In this appendix we will explore some ways the principle of commitment applies in organizational life, specifically in relation to the personal development and fulfilment of individual members.

Take the case of a person who seems to have a vision that is different to the plans of the organization he or she works for. That person should first share with his or her brothers and sisters in the group and they should as a group seek to find out whether this is indeed of the Lord. If they feel convinced that it is of the Lord, then they should see whether they can justifiably adjust the structure of their group to accommodate that vision.

Some of the most exciting developments in our work in YFC in Sri Lanka have come in this way. God burns into the heart of one member the vision of a certain programme of ministry. The leadership discusses and prays about it. They see it is something which YFC can do and they launch out. The process of deciding is, of course, not always very simple. Sometimes we have had to agonize over the decision and usually changes are made on the original scheme as the wisdom of the body makes its impact. The originator of the scheme may find that difficult to accept, yet soon realizes that the change is an improvement to what he or she had originally envisaged.

This type of flexibility, to accommodate the gifts of the members of a group, is not as alien to modern management thinking as it seems at first. Peter F. Drucker, one of America's most famous experts on management, shows, in his autobiographical *Adventures of a Bystander*, that Alfred Sloane, the legendary head of General Motors, one of America's largest corporations, adopted such an approach to the managing of his team (pages 256–293).

When a group shows concern and sensitivity to the visions and gifts of its workers, it is affirming a very important aspect of what we may call 'body theology'. According to this theology, the body consists of individual members and God has a wonderful plan for both the body and the members. Because it is God's will for the members to be in this body, then his will for the members should harmonize with his will for the body.

If a person is completely fulfilled according to God's perspective then the organization for which he or she works would also be completely fulfilled because of his or her services. This is because God's best for the organization will include in it God's best for the member. But we are talking here about fulfilment according to God's perspective, not human. For the member that may mean that he or she will have to spend a lot of time doing things he or she is not particularly adept at and not fond of doing.

For example, a great preacher may need to write a lot of letters and reports, visit donors of the organization or staff members who are sick, purchase office equipment and do other such things that seem to benefit the organization and not himself. But they *do* benefit the preacher too. One of the biggest problems in the church today is that, with specialization, people in ministry are finding it more and more difficult to integrate the various aspects of the whole counsel of God. They think it is a waste of time for a great preacher to spend time visiting the sick. But such experiences give him a background from which to develop his sermons. His sermons will have relevance and depth because he knows how to minister to the needs of people.

'Pure specialists' may produce materials prolifically and these materials may be of high technical excellence. But they lack the penetrative insights that are needed to truly influence people in the ways of God.

Now let us consider the case of a member of an organization who has preaching gifts that should be used outside the organization as well. The leaders, however, are not enthusiastic. So the member takes these speaking engagements privately without seeking the approval of the leadership. Trips are taken secretly. His ministry support team does not at first know about this significant aspect of his ministry. When they find out there is an unpleasant confrontation. All this contradicts the body theology of ministry.

If this member and the organization adopted the body theology approach, the first thing they would do would be to discuss this vision of a wider ministry. In fact, the initiator of the discussion may be a leader who sees that a member of the group has a potential for a wider ministry. Good leaders often have ambitions for those they lead which surpass the personal ambitions which these people have for themselves. The body then agrees that this is indeed a valid course of action and so they release this person for occasional ministry outside the organization.

Now he does not need to do the ministry secretly, but with the blessings of his leaders. They are proud about his achievements and regard it as part of the missionary outreach of their movement. The leadership helps him decide on which invitations to accept and which to reject. He, on the other hand, may decide that the honouraria given to him should be given back to the movement. He does not say, 'This is my hard-earned money', and keep it to himself. Busy typists in the organization would not be able to earn such money however hard they worked. And in God's sight they are as important. In fact, they may be the ones who wrote to the places where the preacher ministered and made the arrangements for the ministry there.

The movement on the other hand ensures that

the special expenses that are incurred because of this itinerant ministry are met. They may ensure, for example, that he has enough money to phone his family when he is 'on the road' and that he has sufficient books for his study and preparation.

Does not all this hinder the success of the organization that the preacher works for? After all, other organizations and churches are growing because of his input. It would seem to hinder success, if success were viewed from a worldly standpoint, for there may be no 'measurable results' in terms of the growth of the organization because of his services. But according to 'kingdom thinking' this *is* a success for the organization, for here success is measured in terms of how much the kingdom grew because of the organization.

Missionary involvement is an important factor in assessing the success of a church or organization. But much missionary involvement does not result in the measurable growth of the group, though the kingdom of God has grown. Here is another place where, by taking its management principles from the market-place, where the law of competition rules, Christians have become unbiblical. Competition may be suitable for the market-place, but it is heretical when applied to kingdom living. Here different organizations and churches are members of the body of Christ. In the market-place establishments with different owners compete with each other to reap profits. But in the kingdom of God all the establishments have the same owner – God!

It should have become clear that what we are describing here is not a structure with no discipline where anyone can do what he or she wants. There is a very exacting discipline here. That is the discipline of spiritual accountability. This is a much bigger challenge to selfish individualism than a strict organizational structure. It touches not only on those features related directly to the 'job description' of the member, but also on his or her personal life.

We may find that job descriptions and such disciplines which modern management systems have advocated are very useful to us. But these job descriptions are part of and subject to our theology that says that the group of believers is the body of Christ. Often today modern management systems have usurped biblical body theology from its rightful place and taken over as the supreme principle influencing the organizational life of Christian groups.

Sometimes the vision a person has for ministry may be very distant to the goals of the organization. Then it becomes clear that if the originator really believes that he or she should follow this path, he or she will have to leave the group. Ways in which this could be done were discussed in chapter three of this book.

# LIST OF PRINCIPAL TEXTS STUDIED

# COMMENTARIES AND STUDIES ON PROVERBS AND ECCLESIASTES

Citations in this book from the commentaries are identified only by the author's name and are not footnoted. They are taken from the discussion in the commentary of the verse being studied.

Aitken, Kenneth T., *Proverbs* (The Daily Bible Study Series. Edinburgh: The Saint Andrew Press; Philadelphia: The Westminster Press).

Alden, Robert l., *Proverbs* (Grand Rapids: Baker Book House, 1983).

Bridges, Charles, *A Commentary on Proverbs* (Edinburgh and Carlyle: The Banner of Truth Trust, 1987 reprint of 1846 edition).

Eaton, Michael A., *Ecclesiastes* (Tyndale Old Testament Commentaries. Leicester: Inter-Varsity Press, 1983).

Kidner, Derek, *Proverbs* (Tyndale Old Testament Commentaries. Leicester: Inter-Varsity Press, 1964).

Martin, Charles G., 'Proverbs', *The International Bible Commentary* (Edited by F. F. Bruce et. al. Hants: Marshall Morgan and Scott; Grand Rapids: The Zondervan Corporation, 1986).

Scott, R. B. Y., *Proverbs, Ecclesiastes* (The Anchor Bible, Garden City, N. Y.: Doubleday and Co., 1965).

Voorwinde, Stephen, *Wisdom for Today's Issues* (Phillipsburg, N. J.: Puritan and Reformed Publishing Co., 1981).

# BIBLIOGRAPHY

Bruce, F. F., *The Pauline Circle* (Exeter: Paternoster Press, 1985).

Collins, Gary, *How to Be a People Helper* (Santa Ana: Vision House Publishers, 1976).

Davis, Ron Lees, *Gold in the Making* (Nashville: Thomas Nelson Publishers, 1983).

Drucker, Peter F., *Adventures of a Bystander* (New York: Harper & Row, Publishers, 1979).

France, R. T., *The Gospel According to Matthew* (Tyndale New Testament Commentaries. Leicester: Inter-Varsity Press, 1985).

Grossman, Eileen, *Mountain Rain* (Singapore: Overseas Missionary Fellowship, 1988).

Inrig, Gary, *Quality Friendship*, (Chicago: Moody Press, 1981).

Lewis, C. S., *The Four Loves* (London: Geoffrey Bles, 1960).

Morris, Leon, *Reflections on the Gospel of John*, Vol. 1, (Grand Rapids: Baker Book House, 1986).

Pollock, J. C., *Hudson Taylor and Maria* (Bromley: STL Books and Eastbourne: Kingsway Publications, 1983 reprint of 1962 edition).

Sayer, George, *Jack: C. S. Lewis and His Times* (San Fransisco: Harper & Row, Publishers, 1988).

Seamand, David, *Healing for Damaged Emotions* (Amersham: Scripture Press, 1986).

Yankelovich, Daniel, *New Rules: Searching for Self-fulfilment in a World Turned Upside Down* (New York: Random House, 1981).